PEARL BRADSHAW
Princess of Hotham

STEPHEN WHITESIDE

First published by Busybird Publishing 2025

Copyright © 2025 Stephen Whiteside

ISBN:
Paperback: 978-1-923216-96-9
Ebook: 978-1-923216-97-6

This work is copyright. Apart from any use permitted under the *Copyright Act 1968*, no part of this publication may be reproduced, stored in a retrieval system or transmitted in any form or by any means, electronic, mechanical, photocopying, recording or otherwise, without the prior written permission of Stephen Whiteside.

The information in this book is based on the author's experiences and opinions. The author and publisher disclaim responsibility for any adverse consequences which may result from use of the information contained herein. Permission to use any external content has been sought by the author. Any breaches will be rectified in further editions of the book.

Cover Image: Pearl Bradshaw seated on Eric Johnson's sledge. The man on the far right is Eric Johnson. The man standing behind Pearl is her husband, Jim.

Cover design: Fiona Sinclair

Layout and typesetting: Busybird Publishing

Busybird Publishing
2/118 Para Road
Montmorency, Victoria
Australia 3094
www.busybird.com.au

*...there were two princes running resorts in Australia.
There was George Day at Charlotte Pass,
and Jim Bradshaw at Hotham.*

Martin Romuld
*Norwegian born skiing champion and SEC (Kiewa scheme)
hydroelectric engineer (quoting Len Becham, another skier)*

*I think they were the first successful people (to manage the
Hotham Heights Chalet)...Jimmy Bradshaw and his wife.*

Mick Hull
Skiing legend

To Maggie

Contents

Introduction		1
1	A Crate of Eggs	5
2	A Well-Oiled Machine	7
3	'Tea and toast' for 'Ding'	10
4	A Box of Flowers	11
5	Harold Clapp and the Bermaline Brown	17
6	A Frozen Pipe	18
7	'Water, water, everywhere...'	19
8	A Specimen of Gold	20
9	"We could have used that..."	21
10	Mr Spargo Takes the Onions	22
11	Fire!	23
12	Serviceton	28
13	The Second Fire	31
14	Loch and Chops	35
15	Bogong Moths - Out on the Prowl!	36
16	Cook Trouble	36
17	Calling in the Union	38
18	Lettuces	39
19	Some Big Carrots	40
20	God and Mr Whatmore	41
21	"You've had quite enough, Jim!"	42
22	A 'Useful' on the Plonk	43
23	Hot Pies, Sandwiches, and Billies of Tea	45
24	"We should have followed Tiger!"	46
25	Tiger and Bill	48
26	The Meat Party	49
27	A Sulky Skier	50
28	Another Quiet Evening	51
29	Weather Balloons and Theodolites	52
30	Lindsay's Nightmares	53
31	Wombat Woes	54
32	A Brief Dip	55
33	Opening the Road	56
34	Return of the Horses	57
35	An Early Road Closure	59
36	A Hot Water Bottle for Joany	60

37	Sleeping with the Maids	61
38	Looking After the Horses	63
39	The Last Little Patch	64
40	Butter Coupons	65
41	The Porridge Problem	66
42	A Visit to Mr Spargo's Mine	67
43	Caught in a Snowstorm	68
44	School for Peter	70
A Closing Word		73

The People — 76

Vic Wraith — 77
'Ding' Dyason — 77
Kath Magill — 79
Bill Spargo — 81
Joyce Brockhoff — 84
'Mr Whatmore' — 85
Harold Brockhoff — 86
Bruce Wenzel — 88
Lindsay Salmon — 89
Noel and Joan Dickson — 93
Eric Johnson — 95
Vic Lawler — 96

The Places — 97

The Red Robin Mine — 99
The Bogong High Plains — 100
Wallaces Hut — 101
Cope Hut — 102

The 1939 Bushfires — 103

Peter Bradshaw - "Young Man of the Mountains" — 107
Photo Credits — 109
Bibliography — 111
Acknowledgements — 113
About the Author — 114
Previous books by Stephen Whiteside — 115

Introduction

In 1987, I began to interview people who had known Bill Spargo and/or Evelyn Piper in my quest to find out as much as possible about the occupants of Spargo's Hut, near Mt Hotham. I began with a handful of people. Each of these suggested one or two further people I should talk to, as did they in turn, and slowly my network grew. These interviews became the backbone of my book, 'Snow, Fire and Gold - the story of Bill Spargo and Evelyn Piper's life in the Australian mountains.'

One such thread ran as follows. I rang Elyne Mitchell, author of the famous children's book, 'The Silver Brumby.' She was also a pioneering skier. Elyne referred me to another early skier, Joan Dickson, who referred me to yet another skiing pioneer, Mick Hull. Mick referred me to the Norwegian born skiing champion and hydroelectric engineer, Martin Romuld. Martin suggested I talk to Pearl Bradshaw. Pearl and her husband, Jim, had managed the Hotham Heights Chalet from 1937 - 1945, a total of nine consecutive winters. This period spanned both the devastating bushfires of 1939, which burnt almost two million hectares of the state of Victoria and cost the lives of 71 people, and the Second World War.

I interviewed Pearl on 11th June 1987, in her home in the outer northern Melbourne suburb of Bundoora. (Jim had died six years earlier, at the age of 72.) Reflecting on the interview afterwards, I realised that her story was intrinsically fascinating - she had much more to offer than simply providing insights into the life of Bill Spargo. With this in mind, I returned to interview her a second time on 9th November 1987. These two interviews provided the material for this book, and can be found online at snowfireandgold.com.au. (Jim and Pearl also managed the Feathertop Bungalow in 1935 and 1936. I am kicking myself now for failing to ask her anything about these years at all! It wasn't hard to imagine what it must have been like, though.)

Pearl explained that the War had had no effect on occupancy rates at the Chalet. It remained fully booked all the time. The Mt Buller Chalet burnt down in July 1942 and Falls Creek did not yet exist, so for much of this time the Hotham Heights Chalet was the only significant accommodation available in the Victorian ski fields. (Mt Buffalo was only really suitable for beginners.)

I have fictionalised these stories slightly, but not to the extent of changing anything fundamentally. I have used Pearl's original words as much as possible, and have occasionally quoted her directly. The names are real, the only exception being that of 'Jack' the 'Useful.' I have included the map I drew for 'Snow, Fire and Gold', as the geography is essentially the same. In the course of writing this book, I have also drawn heavily from the pages of 'Schuss', the (mostly) monthly newsletter of the Ski Club of Victoria that ran from 1935 - 61.

I found Pearl Bradshaw to be a great interview subject. She spoke loudly and clearly, and had a good memory. She had strong opinions, but they were all well-reasoned and fair. I found her stories fascinating. I hope you do too.

Introduction

Victorian Railways photo of Mt Hotham and Hotham Heights Chalet

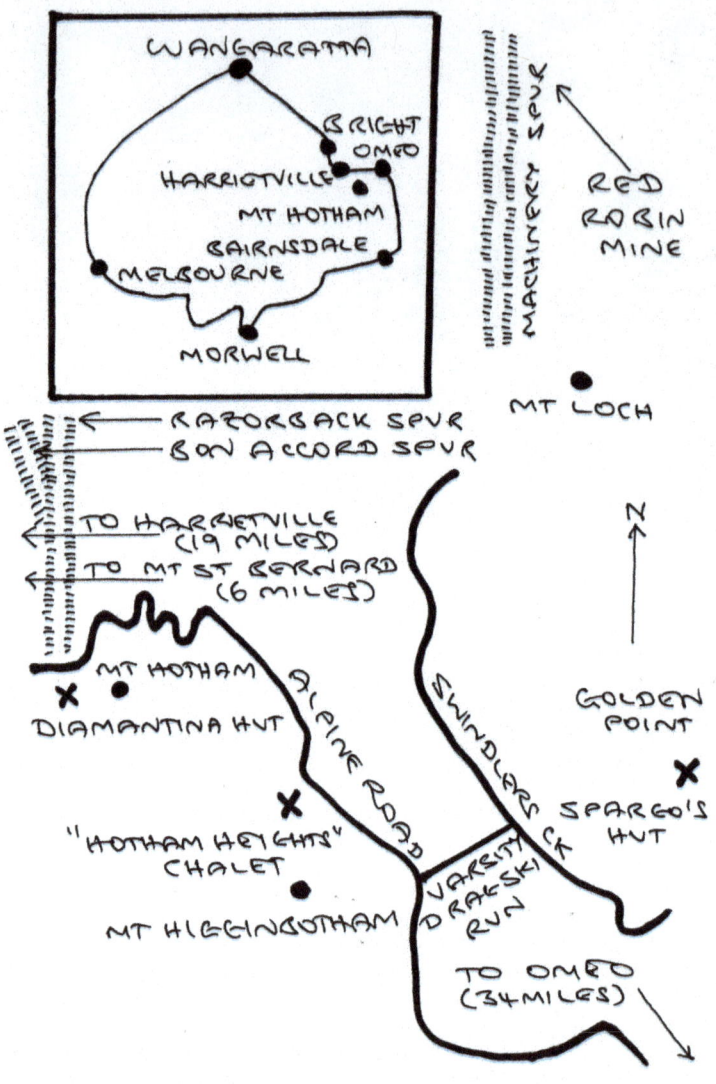

NB: These maps are little more than rough sketches, and should not be relied upon for the purposes of navigation.

1
A Crate of Eggs

The journey from Harrietville had been uneventful. Vic Wraith started to relax as he left the Alpine Road and turned into the short drive that led up to the front of the Chalet. The load was a little more fragile than usual today. Perched high on top was a crate of eggs - six trays with two dozen on each, twelve dozen in total. As he put his foot on the brake at the end of the journey, the truck stopped a little more suddenly than he was expecting. He watched in dismay as the crate, having sailed over the top of the cabin, swept down in front of the bonnet and landed with a crash on the ground! Nooo...! And he had tried to be so careful!

*

Pearl took it in good humour. Besides, they relied on Vic in so many ways, it would not pay to get him offside. They ate scrambled eggs for a long time after that!

Victorian Railways photo of the original Hotham Heights Chalet

Alterations..
and
Improvements
at
"Hotham Heights"
MT. HOTHAM

A NEW ski room, with a concrete floor, has been erected as an annexe to the house. The ski room, containing racks for ski, a waxing stove and a work bench, will form the entrance to the house in winter.

The drying room has been considerably enlarged, and the heating system improved. Extra and more convenient facilities for clothing have also been provided.

The bathrooms have been completely rebuilt. With the septic tank system of sewerage, internal lavatories, and improved hot water system, this section of the house is as up-to-date as modern plumbing can make it.

Mr. and Mrs. J. Bradshaw, who have managed "The Bungalow," Mt. Feathertop, during the past two seasons, are now in charge at "Hotham Heights." They will be assisted during the winter by Mr. W. B. Spargo, who has resided in the vicinity of Mt. Hotham for many years.

Mr. and Mrs. H. Richards are now in charge at "The Bungalow," Mt. Feathertop.

Mr. E. G. Stewart, the Snowline Representative of the Victorian Government Tourist Bureau, will be located at the Harrietville Post Office. He will facilitate the transport arrangements and act as guide, when required, for all visitors to Mt. Hotham, Mt. Feathertop or Mt. St. Bernard.

Before commencing their journey, however, intending visitors (whether they travel by rail or by road) should consult the Victorian Government Tourist Bureau, Queen's Walk, Melbourne; 11 Martin Place, Sydney; 131 King William Street, Adelaide; 204 Adelaide Street, Brisbane; or 8th Street, Mildura.

Issued by the Betterment and Publicity Board,
Victorian Railways, Melbourne.

June, 1937   Victorian Railways Print.   2905—37

Leaflet inserted into Schuss, June 1937

2
A Well-Oiled Machine

Pearl smiled as the young waitresses carried plates of bacon and eggs, grilled chops and hot toast out to the guests. The staff were working well together, and the guests were contented and well behaved. Most of them were finishing their porridge, if they had not already done so, and the bowls were being stacked tidily in the kitchen, ready for washing.

Pearl stood back and allowed herself a moment to reflect. They had come a long way, she and Jim. Those early Depression years had been frightening times for a young couple just starting out in life. She had never had any doubt that the two of them would make a go of it, but the future had been a totally blank sheet, nonetheless. Jim had been out of work at the end of the Depression. Then he had found work on the burgeoning pine plantations near Bright. It offered a steady income, but it was pitifully low, and the work, planting trees, was tedious and hard. He had also done some work as a driver at Mt Buffalo, employed by the Victorian Railways. When the offer had come to manage the Bungalow at Mt Feathertop, also owned by the Railways, they had leapt at the opportunity.

It too, however, had proved extremely difficult. That big corrugated iron building in the heart of the snow country was like an ice box. Everything about it was difficult. The facilities were poor. It wasn't well organised. It was impossible to keep warm. Two seasons there had been more than enough.

The offer of moving to Hotham had been sold to them as a big step up. As it turned out, that was right. The solid stone building with its huge fireplace was so much more comfortable. Its isolation also proved to be an advantage. People could just stagger up the Bungalow Spur at all hours from Harrietville and crash at the

Bungalow. Riding on horseback up the Bon Accord Spur, and then walking over the snow up and over Mt Hotham, and down to the Chalet, was a far more challenging proposition. It required teamwork, and good organisation. That made it predictable - something you could work with comfortably.

Her thoughts returned to the present moment. It was always a bit of a scramble to clean up after breakfast and have lunch ready in time, but it looked as though they were pretty much on target today. Lunch wouldn't be a big meal, but the skiers would still have the choice of a couple of soups, followed by an entree, and then perhaps a serve of steak and kidney pie with mashed potatoes. Dinner would be bigger - again a choice of soups, followed by a choice of two roasts, and then a choice of two or three sweets. They would come in with big appetites - that much could be relied upon. They spent much more time walking up the slopes than they ever spent sliding down them. A couple of runs was about all most could manage in a single morning, and the same again in the afternoon. They were very well fed, but their appetites were more than up to the challenge. Fair dinkum, you could keep yourself busy just keeping these bellies full, but there was so much more to do. Still, Pearl wasn't complaining. She and Jim loved a challenge and, so far at least, it appeared they were meeting it!

Mt Hotham with the original Hotham Heights Chalet in the foreground

The original Chalet, with snow gum logs stacked against it

3
'Tea and toast' for 'Ding'

'Ding' Dyason strolled cheerfully into the dining room, though her manner was somewhat resigned.

"I'll have my tea and toast!"

She knew the rules well enough. You had to be in the dining room before 8.15 to get a cooked breakfast. After 8.15 it was 'tea and toast' only. After 8.30 it was nothing. She also knew Pearl and Jim well. Rules were enforced. They were not made to be broken.

'Ding' always found it difficult to get ready in time for a cooked breakfast, but there was no point in complaining. Tea and toast were a lot better than nothing. There was no limit to the number of pieces she could have and, after all, it wouldn't be long until lunch time, and that would be a cooked meal!

4
A Box of Flowers

As she struggled up the last final pull to the summit from Diamantina Hut, Kath Magill questioned the wisdom of having gently placed a bulky box of spring flowers in the top of her pack. It was not easy to secure it without damaging it with the straps, and it had meant taking a little less clothing than she otherwise might have.

It can't have been an easy life that Pearl Bradshaw had chosen. She was a young woman like herself, and here she was, for months on end, at the beck and call of all the skiers, stuck in this icy wilderness, devoid of any colour save the bright blue of the rare sunny day. No doubt she had been born with fewer opportunities than Kath herself. Still, she was always cheerful, never complained, worked hard and efficiently and, together with her husband, Jim, provided an environment for skiing that could not be bettered. It was a small enough gesture - a few violets, hyacinths, and others - to place in a vase on the mantelpiece of the lounge room, or in her bedroom if she preferred. She was sure the smile of delight and surprise on Pearl's face would more than justify the inconvenience of having carried the awkward box up the mountain.

The Refreshment Services Branch of the Victorian Railways controlled the Hotham Heights Chalet during the years that Pearl and Jim Bradshaw were there. The Railways were also in charge of the Chalet at Mt Buffalo and the Bungalow at Mt Feathertop. Sir Harold Winthrop Clapp (1875 - 1952) was the chairman of the Victorian Railways Commissioners from 1920 - 1939. He was born in St Kilda, Melbourne, but his parents were both American. His father came to Australia as a young man, and had a successful career in public transport in Victoria - Cobb & Co (horse-drawn carriages), horse-drawn omnibuses, and cable trams. Harold followed in his father's footsteps. After completing his schooling in Australia, he travelled to America in 1900. He worked there for twenty years, mostly in senior positions in railway companies. However, in 1920, now in his mid-forties, he successfully applied for the position of Victorian Railways Commissioners chairman and returned to Australia. Nevertheless, he never lost his American accent. He was a dynamic personality, introducing many reforms. He was keen to improve amenities for passengers and arranged for the Victorian Railways to have their own butchery, bakery and poultry farm. He opened a citrus fruit kiosk at Flinders Street Station in 1924. He was fond of slogans, such as

"Citrus fruit is nature's way
To keep you fit for work and play."

He also promoted dried fruit, and had a particular passion for raisin bread.

However, he had his critics. He was mocked for his passion for cleanliness. He had a somewhat brusque manner, and often ended interviews prematurely with the sharply spoken sentence "I'm not hearing you."

Clapp was keen to promote country Victoria and primary producers, as this would increase the demand for freight trains. He developed a large range of publicity posters, employing the leading graphic artists of the day, such as the German born Gert Sellheim. He resigned from the Victorian Railways in June 1939. However, he continued to work in a range of senior positions involving public transport, almost until his death. He was knighted in 1941. Victorian Railways' first diesel-electric locomotive was named the 'Harold W. Clapp.'

Sir Harold Clapp

Victorian Railways promotional posters by German-Australian graphic artist Gert Sellheim (this page and the following)

Victorian Railways promotional poster

5
Harold Clapp and the Bermaline Brown

Pearl received word that Harold Clapp would be paying them a visit. He was having a holiday at the Mt Buffalo Chalet, and planned to come over to Hotham for a day. Pearl turned to her recipe book, and chose Bermaline Brown Bread to bake for him.

It was a big hit. Clapp told Pearl it was the nearest thing to Boston Brown Bread he'd had since he'd left Boston!

6
A Frozen Pipe

Jim sighed deeply. No water was coming out of the tap. That only meant one thing - the pipe had frozen and burst. It was a long length of pipe, running from the well down to the spring at the head of the Dargo. The pipe that ran from the well down to the Chalet was much shorter, and had been placed underground. This prevented it from freezing, but the other pipe was too long to bury. Hopefully the blockage would be near the top, but it was just as likely to be at the other end. No matter where it was, it was a pig of a job - cutting out the length of broken pipe and fitting a replacement. More often than not his hands froze, even with gloves on. Reluctantly he donned boots, overcoat, hat and gloves, and walked out into the bitter cold to face the music. Oh, the joys of Chalet management!

7
'Water, water, everywhere...'

Pearl took young Peter out of the bath and wrapped him up in a towel. Water was so scarce! As soon as she had dressed him and placed him in his cot, she would fetch his clothes and wash them in the bathwater. Then the girls would come and fetch the bath and take it into the kitchen, where they would use the bathwater to wash the kitchen floor. They were all just relying on that one little well. Surely there was a better way of supplying water to the Chalet. They could only even flush the toilet twice a day!

8
A Specimen of Gold

Pearl walked along the little creek beside Mr Spargo. He bent down, picked up a small specimen of gold, and handed it to her. After admiring it, she handed it back to him.

"No, just put it back down again."

"What? You're not just going to leave it there?"

"Yes, of course. How else would I be able to remember where I had found it?"

9
"We could have used that..."

They all got a fright when it exploded. Bang!

Pearl always had plenty of yeast on hand for baking bread. She had placed a small bottle on the mantelpiece. She had meant to move it, but had forgotten. Now, with the heat from the stove, it had exploded.

Bill was the first to react - sober as a judge, as always.

"That was good yeast. We could have used that."

Pearl had to bite her lip to stop from laughing out loud. It would not do to offend Mr Spargo. All the same, tears started to run down her cheeks. She quickly brushed them away.

Poor old Mr Spargo, thought Pearl to herself. That said so much. He just hated to waste anything. The bottle hadn't even been full.

"We could have used that..." Pearl ran the words through her mind again. Well, it was too late to use it now. It was everywhere!

10
Mr Spargo Takes the Onions

Pearl looked at the onions. It was a shame that they had been allowed to sprout. It was always hard to get the catering exactly right. They would be too bitter to eat now, though. She would have to throw them out.

Bill could see what she was up to.

"Would you mind if I kept those onions, Mrs Bradshaw?"

"Yes, of course, Mr Spargo. Take as many as you want."

He took them all.

Golly, thought Pearl to herself. He must be very hard up to want to eat that lot!

11
Fire!

The red glow shone brightly against the night sky. It had moved significantly since the night before. Jim and Pearl had been climbing Little Higgy for several nights now, monitoring the progress of the fire over to the east, on the Bogong High Plains. It looked as though it had passed them by. Tomorrow Pearl would go for a ride! It had been a tense few days. It would be good to get out and stretch her limbs.

*

The sky turned black as night. It was only 4 o'clock. Pearl had been out riding all day with her father and their young female staff member. Now they were on their way home. But which way was home? In the darkness, it was impossible to know. They trusted to their horses, and they didn't let them down, taking them unerringly back to the Chalet. Clearly, though, the fire was still with them. They unsaddled the horses and put them in the yard, but left the sliprails down so that they could leave if they wished.

Jim and Pearl began to make preparations. They filled the bath with water and gathered a pile of wet blankets. Of course, they were under no direct threat themselves. The Chalet was made of double thickness stone walls. The windows, too, were double - inner windows that opened up and down, and outer windows that swung out. Still, it paid to be careful.

At six thirty they sat down for dinner - Pearl, Jim, Pearl's parents, and the young woman. Nine months old Peter was nearby in his bassinette. They had barely begun to eat when they heard a great roar come up the side of the mountain, out of the Dargo.

Jim sprinted up to the attic to make sure everything was all right. The phone rang. Pearl answered it. It was the woman from the

Omeo switchboard, asking after them. Pearl began to tell her that everything was fine. Jim came racing down again.

"The attic's on fire! We've got to leave!"

No wonder the roar was so loud. It was coming from inside the building!

Pearl quickly changed her tune.

"It looks like we've got to go. Jim says the house is on fire. We've got to leave!"

She slammed down the receiver, and grabbed young Peter from his bassinette. Sparks were flying through the windows as if there had been no glass in them at all.

They dashed out of the building. Jim remembered an old well in the side of the hill. It was their best chance. First, though, they had to negotiate a barbed wire fence. Jim held the wire up to create a gap for Pearl.

"Quick, climb through here!"

She panicked.

"I can't! I know I can't get through that!"

He cast around for other ideas. The sliprails were down at one end, as they had left them. They were now on fire, but it was her only chance.

"Can you jump over these?"

Pearl didn't hesitate. One leap, and she was over, Peter still clutched tightly in her arms.

There was a small wooden house over the well. They opened the door and raced inside, collapsing on the ground. The door held a small window but, like the windows of the Chalet, it soon shattered. Pearl and the young woman quickly fell into a routine. They dipped a blanket into the well, and soaked it thoroughly. When they heard the next roar coming up the valley, they held it up to the broken glass. It would be bone dry in seconds. From time to time, they also climbed into the water for short periods.

At around 3 am, they noticed that Peter was very quiet. Up until then, he had been screaming non-stop. Pearl shook him gently to make sure he was OK. He woke up and started screaming again! From time to time they could hear the bell of their dairy cow, Carey, and wondered how she was faring.

At dawn they ventured out once more. The fire had passed through. They quietly picked their way through the smouldering ruins. They had lost everything. Money. Jewellery. Clothes. All their possessions. Peter's moneybox had melted into a globule of metal. At first they thought some of the tinned food might have survived, but it rattled inside its metal container. There was no sign of Carey.

Three of their five horses - Judy, Trixie and Patrick - were still in the horse yard, where they had left them. Their eyelids and manes were singed, but they had survived. Star and 'Hectic Harry' were nowhere to be seen.

They waited until midday, but realised that the longer they waited without food, the weaker they would become. They couldn't even be sure that anybody knew of their plight. They decided they had better start walking out. They only got as far as the Loch spur, however, before they were met by Vic Wraith in his truck. He had another man with him. They had left Harrietville at daylight. It had taken them seven hours to reach them, throwing dead cattle off the road, and cutting through burning logs. The woman on the Omeo switchboard had relayed her concerns to the Victorian Railways. Bert Keown from the Refreshment Services Branch had contacted Vic, and requested his assistance.

On their way back down to Harrietville, they came across Carey and her calf, walking along the side of the road. How wonderful to see her again! Coming to St Bernard, they picked up Barney Rush and his family. They had survived the burning of the Hospice, and Vic had left them by the side of the road to be picked up on his return.

Pearl and Jim stayed in Harrietville for a couple of nights before being taken down to Melbourne. The cattlemen told them that Star and Harry had been found dead. They said that they had died quickly, though, running blindly into trees and breaking their necks. Whether that was true, or whether the cattlemen had simply been trying to be kind, Pearl never knew.

Peter's little arms were covered in spark burns. It took days of bathing for Pearl to completely wash the soot out of his hair. Pearl and Jim both suffered from very sore and inflamed eyes. Jim's were so bad he had to seek medical attention. Peter's eyes, however, were unaffected. Pearl wondered if the tears from all his crying - he had screamed throughout almost the entire ordeal - had saved his eyes. Pearl carried a leaf-shaped scar on one of her arms for many years after.

Pearl and Jim would soon return to Hotham, but there would be no fresh milk again. It would be powdered milk only from then on.

They had not known about the fire in the Buckland valley. It had travelled east and come up behind the Chalet. Smoke haze prevented Pearl and Jim from seeing whether Mr Spargo's hut was still standing. Pearl assumed that he had perished.

Hotham Heights Chalet after the 1939 fire

Fire!

I took this photo in 2015, near where the old Chalet stood. Could this be the ruins of the well where the Bradshaws sheltered from the fire?

12
Serviceton

Pearl groaned and rolled over. She had set the alarm for midnight. They had had a nap in the middle of the day, but it never seemed to make much difference. They'd been working in this routine for several weeks now, but it hadn't got any easier.

Saturday nights were a challenge. The train from Adelaide would arrive at 1 am. The travellers, mostly from Wolseley and the surrounding towns, would pour off the train with one thing on their mind, and one thing only - to consume as much alcohol as possible before catching the train from Melbourne to take them back home again forty-five minutes later. They were supposed to only serve them alcohol for the first twenty minutes, but that was not an easy rule to enforce. Besides, it's amazing how much alcohol a person can pack away in twenty minutes if they really set their mind to it! A bowl of soup and a plate of roast beef and vegetables was available if they so desired, but few did.

This sure was a long way from Mt Hotham. Still, they were Victorian Railways employees, and they would do as they were told, and go where they were sent. How could they have imagined twelve months ago that they would find themselves here, barely a stone's throw from the South Australian border?

Pearl missed the bonhomie of the skiing fraternity, but there was nothing that could be done about it, and Mr Keown had assured them that they would be back at Hotham just as soon as the new Chalet was ready - and hopefully in time for the opening of the ski season. They would just have to tough it out for another couple of months. They'd also been promised a holiday before they went back. That would be much appreciated - their feet had barely touched the ground since that dreadful night at Hotham.

Enough of this self-reflection. There was work to be done, and time was slipping away. Jim, she could tell, had fallen back to sleep. She gave him a sharp elbow in the ribs.

"Come on, Jim. Time to get up!"

Victorian Ski Resorts

By P. E. (Mick) Hull

Hotham Chalet, 1939

PHOENIX-LIKE from the ashes a new Hotham Heights has arisen and what a building, with a full house of hard-to-please skiers. Unreservedly they heartily congratulate the Railways Department for the excellent job that has been produced, despite severe difficulties.

For the new Hotham is modern. Electric light, central heating, a sun-porch, hot water in bathrooms, only a soap-throw from comfortable bedrooms, a kitchen to serve 100, ski-racks fitted with arch preservers, a glass-walled dining-room and lounge, carpets thick enough to make one think of soft snow runs—these are only a few of its appointments. And Jim Bradshaw and his staff had things running as if the house had been established for years.

The completion of the building is a triumph to Mr. Keown of the Victorian Railways Refreshment Service Department and his staff, and to the Way and Works branch organisation, who executed the work. For the difficulties were many—time was short, transport over the Alpine road to 6,000 feet was difficult, skilled labour was in heavy demand, low temperatures affected concrete work, finance had to be studied carefully, and so on, right through the autumn months. However, the weather gods were kind to their efforts, and the last loads were delivered only a day or so before the road closed for the season. The race against winter was won. Then, as the workmen left the finished job, the snow we had long been expecting arrived plentifully to provide excellent ski-ing conditions. Needless to say, the house was fully booked for the season, and deservedly so. Three times this accommodation would be too little.

13
The Second Fire

Pearl stood up and arched her back, hands on her hips. It was hard enough getting down on all fours to light one fire, without having to stand up, and then get down again to light the second one. The Railways had done a superb job of getting the new Chalet up in place and ready - well, almost ready - in time for the 1939 ski season. Nobody could deny its style and modernity, but clearly it had not been designed by a woman. Certainly, the kitchen hadn't. Placing the stoves out in the middle of the room was odd, but she supposed she could get used to that easily enough. But why did there have to be separate fires for the two stoves? Couldn't one fire have served them both? It wasn't as though they didn't need them both operating all the time. Nor was it the case that her time wasn't precious. This just seemed like somebody's idea of a wicked prank! She shook her head and walked around to the other side. The second fire was not going to light itself.

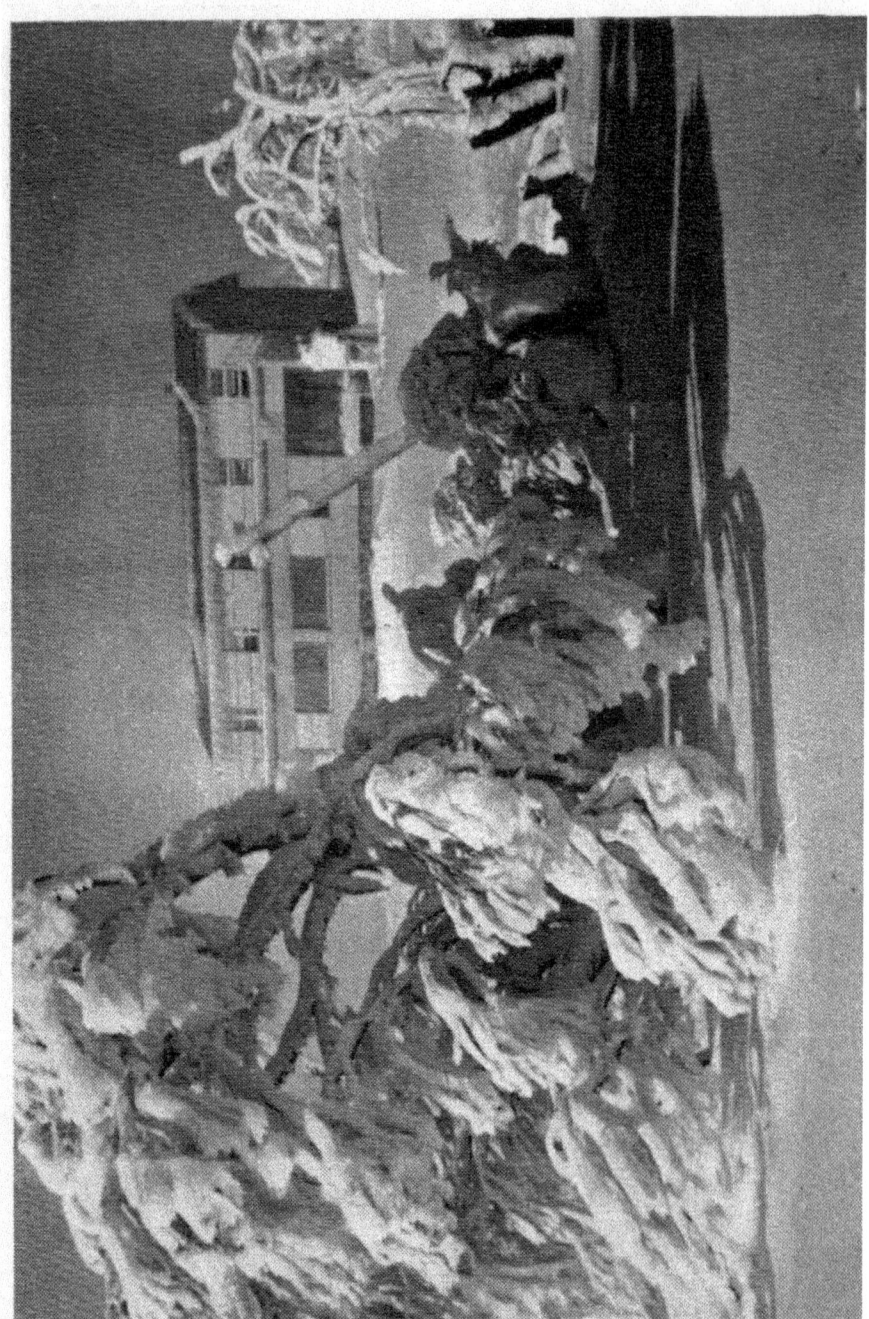

The rebuilt Hotham Heights - view from the north

The rebuilt Hotham Heights - view from the east (front)
(Note the child's swing by the front door.)

ON THE WAY TO MT. LOCK.
Photo. O. H. McCutcheon.

Schuss, January 1938

14
Loch and Chops

Joyce Brockhoff could sense it was a lovely day before she even opened her eyes. She could feel the sunshine on her eyelids. A brief peek out the window confirmed her first impression - a clear blue sky! Her heart thrilled at the prospect of the day that lay before her. There would probably still be a stiff breeze, but that was just part of the scenery. She dressed quickly and walked out to face the world. She hunted Pearl down quickly.

"Loch and chops?" she asked excitedly.

Pearl knew exactly what she meant. This was a well-worn path. She knew how much Joyce loved skiing with friends out to Mt Loch on a day like this. She would pack them raw chops (and perhaps a few sausages), bread and butter, tea and sugar, and they would all set off on another great adventure. The summit of Mt Loch offered magnificent views - why, it was some twenty odd feet higher than Mt Hotham itself! Once there, they would light a fire and grill their meat. It just felt like paradise to Joyce when the warm juice trickled down your chin!

"No worries. Just let me know how many of you are going."

Joyce quickly started doing the rounds of the other guests, to see how many would be joining her. No doubt there would be quite a few!

15
Bogong Moths - Out on the Prowl!

She heard them before she saw them - a loud "Whirr!"

It was after dark, and Pearl happened to be outside. She covered herself up as best she could. The moths covered her like a blanket. She knew from experience that the best thing to do was simply stand still, and not panic. They would come in waves, but ten or fifteen minutes later, they would all be gone.

16
Cook Trouble

"She ordered two chops and one steak!"

"So?"

"Well, you've cooked her one chop and two steaks! That's not what she ordered, and it's not what I told you, either!"

The two sisters (one the cook, the other a waitress) were going at it hammer and tongs beside the bain-marie. Joan, the cook, had not caused any problems until Marg had arrived. Since then, it had been nothing but trouble. The two clearly did not get on.

*

"I've got three!"

"I've got five!"

It was lunch time, Sunday. The guests were competing to see who had the most cloves. Pearl was dying with embarrassment. The previous Sunday had seen the opposite problem. She had asked Joan to put some cloves in the apple pie. It had been an awkward conversation. At first Joan had resisted the idea, but eventually she agreed to do so. However, when the pie had been served, there were no cloves to be seen. This week Pearl had asked her again. Clearly, this was her revenge. She must have just loaded up a handful and thrown them in!

*

Marg's face was creased with alarm as she spoke to Pearl.

"Mrs Bradshaw, Joan has threatened to cut her throat!"

Pearl was sick of all this emotional blackmail.

"Good-oh, I hope she makes a good job of it!"

Marg was shocked.

*

"What do you think you're doing here?

Pearl addressed Joan sharply.

"I've come to cook dinner."

"Well, you can get back to your room, because I'm going to cook the dinner."

Earlier in the day, Joan had told Pearl that she was not going to cook any more. Pearl had called her bluff, saying that was fine, she would do all the cooking herself. She had made lunch, now here was Joan offering to cook dinner. She was not indispensable, and the point needed to be drummed home. Pearl proceeded to cook the dinner.

The following morning, Pearl walked into the kitchen at about half past six. Joan had the breakfast well and truly on the way. Clearly, Pearl had made her point.

17
Calling in the Union

"I'm going to report you to the union!"

Pearl was disgusted with the triviality of the complaint. Most of the staff knew what they were in for before they arrived, but with the outbreak of the War it had been more difficult to recruit their own, and the Railways had had to send them up some young women.

"I don't know how you're going to do that. They don't even know you exist up here."

18
Lettuces

Pearl stood back and admired the little patch of lettuces that she had planted near the Chalet. They had begun to grow nicely. It was very early days but, with the whole of summer stretching out before them, who knew! It might be possible, even up here, 6,000 feet above sea level, to grow a nice little bunch of lettuces.

*

Pearl stood back and miserably surveyed the sorry state of what she had so hoped would be a fine harvest of healthy lettuces. Clearly, summer at 6,000 feet was not the same as summer in the valley! They had had a fall of snow every month for the entire season. Each time the lettuces had begun to look as though they were coming on nicely and there might still be hope, a fresh dump of snow would cook off the outer leaves, and the whole process would have to start all over again. Now, here they were in autumn, and there was only one word to describe their lettuce crop - a failure. Maybe two - a total failure!

19
Some Big Carrots

Pearl stood staring at the scene of devastation before her. It had never occurred to her that little Peter would do this. He had seen that she needed some carrots for cooking, and had offered to fetch them for her. She had asked him to bring some big ones. She and Jim always buried the carrots and parsnips that they brought up from the valley. The cold earth kept them fresh and crisp. This year, for something different, she had also planted some carrot seeds. Perhaps they'd be able to grow their own. Certainly, the early signs had been promising, with tiny little carrot tops poking out through the ground. Peter had returned, however, saying he hadn't been able to find any big ones. When asked how big they were, he had showed with his fingers that they were not very big at all. Suddenly flooded with anxiety, Pearl dashed outside. No! He had pulled every one of the new seedlings out of the ground, trying to find a big carrot! So much for a lovely crop of home-grown carrots this year!

20
God and Mr Whatmore

Pearl and Peter noticed, as they were walking down the road, that the telephone line had come down.

"Who made that line?" Peter asked.

"Mr Whatmore."

"I thought you told me God made everything."

"Oh, yes, that's right. God made it, but Mr Whatmore put it up there."

*

It was a Tuesday evening. Pioneer Tours had brought a party up to spend a night at the Chalet, as they did regularly during the summer months.

Peter addressed one of the guests.

"See all those trees over there?"

"Yes."

"God made every one of those trees, and Mr Whatmore put 'em up."

21
"You've had quite enough, Jim!"

Jim and Pearl sat together in the lounge room of the Chalet, tears of laughter rolling down their cheeks. Jim had had a long day, and he was recounting it now. He had set off early with an unusually animated Bill Spargo for the trip down to Harrietville and Bright. For Jim, it was a routine trip to pick up supplies from the train station at Bright and bring them back to the Chalet. For Bill, however, it was anything but. He had finally proved to his own satisfaction that he had, indeed, 'struck it rich' with the Red Robin reef, and he was off to the pub to celebrate! Not one to drink alcohol as a general rule (let's face it, he hadn't been able to afford it until now!), he had a lot of catching up to do.

Jim had left Bill at the Harrietville pub, and headed off to Bright alone. There were quite a few jobs he had to attend to, and it was several hours by the time he was back in Harrietville to pick up Bill and head back to Hotham. He was feeling a little dry himself by then. 'One for the road!' was in order. As he raised the glass to his lips, however, he became aware of a figure approaching him from the side. It was Bill Spargo, staring at him through bloodshot eyes, and swaying slightly from side to side. "I think you've had quite enough, Jim!"

Bill's slurred little speech caused Jim to stiffen for an instant. Then he realised the absurdity of the situation. He put his arm around Bill's shoulder, and downed his glass. "You're quite right, Bill! Let's get going!"

*

Returning to the Chalet, Bill and Jim had carried in the groceries that Jim had bought, together with Bill's bottles of beer. A bottle fell to the concrete floor of the storeroom and smashed. Bill dropped down on all fours, wet his finger, and licked it. "Thank God!" he shouted. "It's only vinegar!" He had since staggered off to bed. He was in no fit state to return to the mine that night!

22
A 'Useful' on the Plonk

"I've solved the riddle, Pearl."

Jim had discovered that some of the grog was missing. Since Bill Spargo had discovered his gold mine he was no longer available to work for them, and they had had to employ other 'usefuls'. Most of them came from the Ovens Valley, but Jack had been sent up from Melbourne by the Railways. He appeared to be reasonably competent, but they could never find him when they needed him.

"I found Jack, too. He's down in the storeroom - blotto!"

"From Horse to Ski at Bon Accord Snow Line, en route to Hotham"

23
Hot Pies, Sandwiches, and Billies of Tea

Clearly, Pearl thought to herself, the cook was in a good mood! This was Saturday, changeover time for the guests. (Most stayed for one week. A few stayed for two, but longer than that was not allowed. Demand on accommodation was too high.) Normally they were only given sandwiches to take with them to eat for lunch at the Bon Accord Hut before mounting the horses and riding down to Harrietville. Today, though, she had baked hot pies for them all - a rare treat!

The scene before her was all hustle and bustle, as the skiers rummaged around for missing items, donned their wet weather gear, and threw their rucksacks on their backs. They were preparing for the journey home...the long climb up Mt Hotham, over the top and down the other side to the Diamantina Hut, along the Razorback to the Bon Accord Spur, and then down that all the way to Harrietville. Somewhere along that journey - probably before they got to the Bon Accord Hut - they would meet the incoming party. There would naturally be exchanges, the sharing of bits of news (if the weather allowed), but these conversations would be brief. The incoming skiers would be keen to reach the Chalet as soon as possible.

A hot cup of tea would be waiting for the outgoing skiers at the Bon Accord Hut. With a bit of luck, there would even be a few leftover sandwiches. (Understandably, the incoming skiers had first claim on these.)

Pearl knew it would be a very different scene later in the afternoon as the incoming skiers, varying enormously in strength and skiing ability, straggled into the Chalet. For now, though, she was caught up in the moments of departure. Changeover day was always a challenge!

24
"We should have followed Tiger!"

They'd had trouble from the start. From the moment she had left the back of her horse and donned her skis, she'd been falling repeatedly and sobbing hysterically. Jim was doing his best to help her up the mountain. He had taken her rucksack from her. Harold Brockhoff and Bruce Wenzel had stayed back to help him, but they couldn't carry her up the mountain. She had to get there under her own steam. To make matters worse, the weather was dreadful - a high wind, and a thick fog. Progress was painfully slow, and Jim was worried they were going to run out of daylight.

*

Halfway down from the summit, they admitted defeat. They had no clear idea where they were, and no strong sense of where they should be going. There was nothing for it. They were going to have dig a snow cave in the side of the mountain, and settle in for the night. Fortunately, they had the mail, including the week's papers. They could line the cave with newspaper. Jim watched in despair as Tiger, their Queensland heeler, took off down the mountain, heading into the Dargo. What a shame to lose him like that. He loved that dog.

*

Pearl paced back and forth anxiously. The incoming party were all safely ensconced in the Chalet - save three. Pearl heard the story of the young woman with no previous skiing experience who had dropped her bundle completely, and was requiring so much assistance. They'd had situations like this before, but everybody had always made it to the Chalet by sundown. This was new territory.

*

When Tiger came bounding down to the Chalet, Pearl greeted him with mixed emotions. it was wonderful to see him, but where were the others?

*

The night seemed to be going on forever. The snow cave was bitterly cold, but it least it protected them from the wind. Suddenly, at about 3 am, the moon came out. The fog had lifted, and they could see the Chalet clearly below them. In fifteen minutes, they were safely back within its walls.

Jim crouched down to greet Tiger as he came bounding up to him. He grabbed him by the ears, and shook his head affectionately from side to side.

"You little rascal! You knew all along, didn't you!"

He looked up to Pearl. "We should have followed Tiger!"

Jim made a mental note. In future, nobody who was completely lacking in skiing experience would be allowed to book a holiday at the Chalet.

25
Tiger and Bill

It was a case of confusion all around.

Firecrackers were exploding nearby. Normally a very placid dog, Tiger had turned on Bill Spargo. Did he think that Bill was attacking young Peter? It was hard to know what was going on. Jim immediately jumped to Bill's defence, and Tiger backed off straight away. No great harm was done, but Bill had had a nasty fright, nonetheless.

Bill and Tiger viewed each other with great suspicion ever after.

26
The Meat Party

Pearl stood with her hands on her hips, looking up towards the summit of Hotham. The meat party was something of a spectacle, and she didn't want to miss it. She and Jim always brought a truckload of meat up before the start of the ski season, but inevitably it ran out well before the end. Then it had to come up the Bon Accord on packhorses. It had to be carried by people from the snowline, though - up and over Hotham, and down to the Chalet. There was never any shortage of manpower. The skiers used to love to assist. Harold Brockhoff was right in the thick of it, as always. She watched with amusement - and mild amazement - as he skied down the mountain towing a sheep behind him. No doubt he had fashioned a rough sledge out of a couple of old skis. Others had various hunks of meat on their shoulders. Jim would have struggled to get the job done with just him and the 'useful'. It was so much easier - and so much more fun! - with all these willing helpers on hand.

Jim Bradshaw

27
A Sulky Skier

It was his problem, it wasn't hers. Pearl was quite confident about that. Here they were serving lunch, and he hadn't moved from his chair all morning. Well, he knew the rules. They all did. If you arrived after 8.30 in the morning expecting breakfast, you would be disappointed. No ifs or buts. Pearl and Jim ran a tight ship. They had to. If they started making exceptions more and more people would start turning up later, and it would become impossible to have lunch ready on time. No, rules were rules. He could sit and sulk for as long as he liked. It would make no difference.

28
Another Quiet Evening

It was almost time to go to bed. The dinner dishes had been washed and put away. Pearl had briefly tried to listen to the news on their little radio. It could only pick up a Tasmanian station, however, and reception was sketchy at the best of times. Above all the background static it hadn't been worth it, and she had turned it off.

The skiers were tired, and quiet. A few were holding little parties in their bedrooms. A few more were relaxing in the lounge room. The usual drinks were being enjoyed - rum and raspberry, rum and cloves, rum and fifty-fifty. A few were drinking whiskey. The ladies were mostly drinking gin. There was never any beer - it was too heavy for the small amount of alcohol it contained!

It was rare for the guests to make much noise in the evenings, or stay up late. They were in bed by midnight at the very latest. Yes, they were a pretty good crowd, these skiers.

29
Weather Balloons and Theodolites

It was all a bit of a mystery to Pearl, but Jim clearly knew what he was doing. After all, he had completed some formal training in meteorology. It certainly kept him busy. First, there were the weather reports that were required to be sent around the country four times a day, at least during the summer months. Then there were the weather balloons. He filled them with gas, released them, and followed them with a theodolite. This allowed him to track their movements both horizontally and vertically, providing important information on wind speed and direction in the higher levels of the atmosphere. Just another reason to be proud of her husband!

Jim Bradshaw working at the weather station - Schuss, October 1945

30
Lindsay's Nightmares

It took Pearl a moment to work out where she was. It must have been the screaming that woke her up. Again. This was the third night this week. Poor Lindsay. He had been sent here by the government for recuperation. They probably thought he stood the best chance living in the country he loved. He must have had a terrible time in Lebanon. Training soldiers to ski sounds like a glamorous job, but no doubt it had been the bright tip of a very dark iceberg. Now here he was, still living in snow, but on the other side of the world. Daylight would come and Lindsay Salmon would sit in a chair, smoking like a chimney and coughing his lungs out, then night would come once more - an endless, harrowing cycle of pain and suffering. Pearl and Jim had agreed they would provide him with all the support he needed for as long as it took. Hopefully he would come good in time.

Members of the 1 Australian Corps Ski School (Sgt Lindsay Sydney Salmon is third from the left)
Memorial reference number: 011406

31
Wombat Woes

"Oh, God, Pearl, I wish we'd come to a bend!"

Jim and Pearl had left Harrietville after sundown for the return journey to Hotham. Once again, they had found themselves stuck behind a wombat - that broad posterior slowly ambling along the road. A quarter of a mile later, Jim's prayer was answered. The beam of the headlights directed the wombat straight ahead, over the bank and down the mountainside. Jim steered around to the right, and quickly picked up speed.

32
A Brief Dip

Crouched now by the fire with a towel wrapped around her, she wasn't quite sure why she had done it. "Because it was there," perhaps. Curiosity. Pearl had taken a swim in the well - the smaller, older well that they no longer used for the Chalet's water supply. A swim? More like a brief dip! She had never been so cold in her life! Well, at least she had it out of her system. Strike it off the list. She wouldn't be doing that again!

33
Opening the Road

Pearl felt a bit sorry for Jim as he gave his back a good stretch before getting into bed. She didn't often feel this way, because Jim was usually well on top of any job that needed to be done. This was just so relentless, though. The snow had all melted off the road except for a couple of large patches. These didn't get a lot of sun, and weren't going to move in a hurry. Jim and Pearl needed to get the road open again as soon as possible and, unfortunately, there was only one way to do it - removing the snow by the shovelful. Jim had been going at it for a week now, but he reckoned it would be another few days before the job would be done.

"Come over here, Jim, and let me give your back a good rub. You poor old thing!"

34
Return of the Horses

The moment Pearl woke up, something did not feel quite right. She lay there listening. What was it? Then it hit her. Of course! It was silent. There was no sound. It must be snowing. She got up and looked out the window. Yes, no doubt about it, it was snowing quite hard.

This threw a spanner in the works. They hadn't expected snow so early in the year. The horses had to be taken down to the valley before the snow started falling. They had been planning to take them down in the next day or so, so had not bothered to replenish the supply of chaff, and now they had nothing. She broke the news to Jim.

"We'll have to get the horses below the snowline, Pearl. They've got to be able to eat."

He sounded as anxious as she was.

*

Jim and Pearl headed off down the Omeo road with the horses. Not until they reached Dinner Plain did they find a suitable area to leave them. They left them there to graze happily, and slowly plodded their weary way back to the Chalet. It was late at night by the time they arrived.

*

The moment Pearl woke up the next morning, she could sense that something was wrong.

"I can hear horses stamping around, Jim."

"Oh, you're mad!"

"I'm sure I can hear horses."

The horses had returned during the night, looking for their regular feed of chaff. There was nothing else for it. Jim and Pearl saddled and haltered the horses straight away and took them down to Harrietville, riding two and leading the others.

35
An Early Road Closure

It seemed crazy for this time of year, but there it was. Two school children from Porepunkah were coming to the Chalet to spend some time with their parents during the May school holidays. The road was blocked from Diamantina Hut, so Jim and Pearl would have to arrange to pick up the children there, and bring them over the top of Hotham. So much snow!

36
A Hot Water Bottle for Joany

Noel Dickson staggered through the front door of the Chalet. The weather was shocking, but he was one of the first of the party to arrive. The knot under his chin that kept his hat in place, and also kept the flaps secured over his ears, was encrusted with ice. Likewise, the laces of his boots. In his exhausted state, the task of undoing them was beyond him. Pearl attended to him while he collapsed on a seat. This was nothing new for her. Indeed, it was routine. Almost all the skiers required assistance of this nature when the weather was bad - which it usually was at this time of year. It was not until the job was largely completed, and Noel had recovered his breath to some extent, that he spoke for the first time.

"Thanks, Pearl. I have another favour to ask. Joany will be here soon. Would you mind putting a hot water bottle in her bed for her?"

Pearl nodded agreeably, though the request struck her as unusual.

"Of course, Noel. I'll be happy to do that for you."

*

Over dinner that night, Pearl shared the day's events with Jim.

"Oh, that Noel Dickson. He's so worried about his Joany. He asked me to put a hot water bottle in her bed for her!"

"I should bloody well hope he would! Do you know, that girl carried her pack and his too! That's why he was in here in time to put a hot water bottle in her bed!"

37
Sleeping with the Maids

"I object to having to sleep with the maids!"

The young woman addressed Pearl angrily. She was a member of the University Ski Club party that had booked the Chalet for two weeks in August. Unfortunately, they had overbooked, and the only available bed was in the "maids'" room.

"Well, it's the only spare bed in the place," Pearl replied. "You either sleep there, or you go down the mountain…and don't think you are paying the maids any compliment by sleeping in their room. They are obliging you by allowing you to sleep in their room!"

There were no further objections from the young woman after that.

Eric Johnson with his horse-drawn sledge

38
Looking After the Horses

It had been another long, hard day, bringing in the new party of skiers. Jim and Pearl lay side by side in bed. It was one of the few times they got to talk to each other to any great extent. If they weren't too tired, it was the best time for reflection.

"I don't know, Pearl. It's a clever idea, putting snowshoes on horses, but it's very hard to watch them floundering around in the snow like they were today."

He paused. Pearl had seen Eric Johnson's horses too, but not as much as Jim. It had looked cruel to her, but this was Jim's domain. He started again.

"I really don't like it. I know the skiers love it, being able to walk in without having to carry their luggage, but I don't care. That is not sufficient justification for cruelty. I think in future, unless we really have to - particularly bad weather, or something like that - I'll tell Eric we don't need him. He won't be happy, but that's just too bad. You have to draw the line somewhere."

"You'll get no argument from me, Jim."

39
The Last Little Patch

Pearl stood on the sundeck of the Chalet and took in the view across to Australia Drift. Yes, it looked as though that little patch was going to make it. The snow on Australia Drift had been melting ever since the end of the last ski season, but it looked as though it wasn't going to disappear completely. Now here we were in May. The air was cold, and a big snow dump was on the way. Soon it would be winter - officially. Unofficially, of course, winter was already well and truly here. There had been a large fall of snow last month, too, but it had been followed by quite a warm period, and she thought the remainder of the snow might have melted then, but it hadn't. There wasn't much of it, but it was definitely there. Snow all year round - that's Mt Hotham for you!

40
Butter Coupons

The War had made catering so difficult. It had been a blow when the government had announced that rations of sugar, butter and tea would be determined by their occupancy rate in March. There was hardly anybody there in March other than them and the staff! Surely, rationing should be based on their winter occupation rates, when they were fully booked. But no, the government would not budge.

What to do? The problem had been partly solved by insisting that guests produce their ration coupons for the time they would be away when they picked up their tickets, but there was still a shortfall. Fortunately, the man in Bright from whom they picked up their groceries had a large family that did not eat butter, and he was happy to give his coupons to the Chalet. That had helped considerably.

41
The Porridge Problem

Pearl stood in the centre of the kitchen, supervising breakfast. The strict rationing of sugar had made it very difficult to find something sweet to place on the guests' porridge. Alternatives had needed to be found. Honey had been good for a while, but then they had run out. Golden syrup had been reasonable, too, for a while, but that had also run out. The snow season was nearly over, but not quite. Something else would have to be found. It looked like it was going to have to be jam. Jam on your porridge! Now, that was strange! Still, nobody complained. They were grateful to have a bowl of porridge at all.

42
A Visit to Mr Spargo's Mine

Pearl stood gasping by the side of the narrow road, teetering on the edge. The steep valley yawned below her, and it was all she could do to stop herself from falling into it. She had not expected to react like this, and had eagerly accepted Mr Spargo's invitation to visit his Red Robin gold mine. All had gone well for a while. She had never seen thick veins of gold in rock before. She had only seen alluvial gold. It looked just like she had imagined it would - better even. She had assumed gold in rock would look a little dull, but it looked just like gold should - bright and shiny!

Then suddenly, out of nowhere, she had become overwhelmed by a sense of being closed in, of being trapped deep in the bowels of the earth. Before she knew what she was doing, she had bolted clean out of that tunnel like a bullet from a gun. It had been fascinating seeing the veins of gold in the rock, but it wasn't something she imagined she would be doing again in a hurry.

43
Caught in a Snowstorm

Pearl crouched forward on her horse's back while the sleet pounded them both from behind. She didn't have any choice in the matter. Her horse had refused to go any further. It had simply stopped, and turned its back to the weather.

It had all started with the mustering. It was time for the famous annual Bogong High Plains cattle muster, and she and one of the housemaids were keen to see the show. They had ridden over to Wallaces Hut, but it was full of cattlemen, so they had left their horses in the yard there, and walked over to Cope Hut to spend the night. It had rained during the night, but in the morning it was very quiet. It was snowing. They had walked back to Wallaces Hut to find that the cattlemen had already kindly saddled their horses. (It did occur to Pearl, though, that it would have been even kinder of them if they had brought the saddled horses over to Cope Hut for them - but they hadn't!)

They had decided that they had better head back to Hotham as quickly as possible, but the weather had continued to deteriorate. Eventually it had turned to wet, sago snow, and the horses had refused to budge. Now here they were, frozen to the spot!

*

The two young women arrived back at Hotham exhausted, and freezing cold. The horses had agreed to start walking again after about half an hour, but the weather had only improved marginally. As Pearl climbed off her horse, she realised the young housemaid was incapable of doing so. Vic Lawler had come out to greet them. He quickly sized up the situation, and helped the young woman down from her horse.

*

The housemaid later swore she would never visit the High Plains again. For Pearl, though, it was experiences like that that made life worthwhile.

44
School for Peter

"We could send him down to Albury, Pearl. You know Albury Grammar is a good school."

"Yes, I know, Jim."

Pearl didn't sound convinced. Peter was now seven years old. By rights, he should have started school last year. The correspondence schooling had been great, but that was nothing more than a stopgap measure. They couldn't put the decision off much longer.

"I just don't want to lose him, Jim. I would miss him...and I'd worry about him."

"Well, if you want to stay with him, we'll all have to leave the mountain. It's as simple as that."

Pearl said nothing, but sat staring at the carpet.

They'd been going around and around in this same tight circle for months now. Sooner or later, they were going to have to make a decision. It wasn't easy, though. They had grown to love their life on the mountain. How would they ever find a job near a school that offered as much excitement, challenge and camaraderie as this? The answer was simple. They wouldn't. Besides, change was always difficult, and good jobs were hard to come by. It wasn't as though they could just step into something else. Then again, they were resilient, and adaptable. The moves to Feathertop, and then Hotham, had proved this, if nothing else. They had also forged a number of good friendships among the rich and powerful - the elite of society. This was not to be snobbish. It was just a simple fact.

Pearl stood up, and walked back and forth across the room several times, her head down. Then she crossed over to the window, and stood gazing out, her back to her husband.

"All right, then, Jim. That's it. We're leaving."

School for Peter

"Swindler's Creek, Hotham"

Schuss, December 1945

A Closing Word

Following their departure from Mt Hotham, the Bradshaws purchased a delicatessen in St Kilda, an inner suburb of Melbourne. The venture did not prove successful, and did not last long. To quote Pearl,

"Oh, gee, I think people that run delicatessens deserve gold medals!"

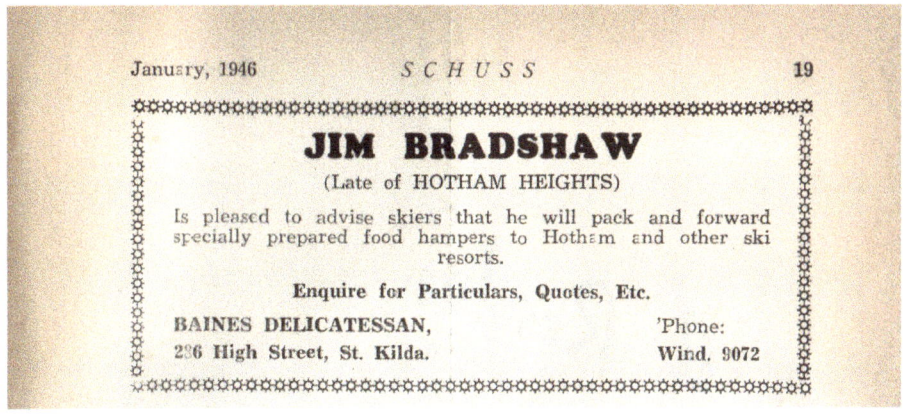

Schuss, January 1946

One of the Hotham skiers was the head of a transport company, George Green and Sons. He asked Jim to work for him. Jim managed their service station, in Park Street, South Melbourne, for many years, until his eventual retirement.

The Hotham Heights Chalet passed through the hands of several managers before Bill and Popsy Harris took it over, with some distinction.

The Chalet was purchased from the Victorian Railways by the Ski Club of Victoria in 1952. It received a license to serve alcohol in 1957, thereby changing its name from Hotham Heights Chalet to Hotham Heights Hotel. (The license was transferred from the St Bernard Hospice which, unlike Hotham Heights, had not been rebuilt following the 1939 fire.) The Chalet eventually burnt down in 1976. I mentioned this to Pearl in 1987. She was surprised and disappointed to hear this news. She was planning a trip to Hotham in the near future, and had been looking forward to seeing the old Chalet again.

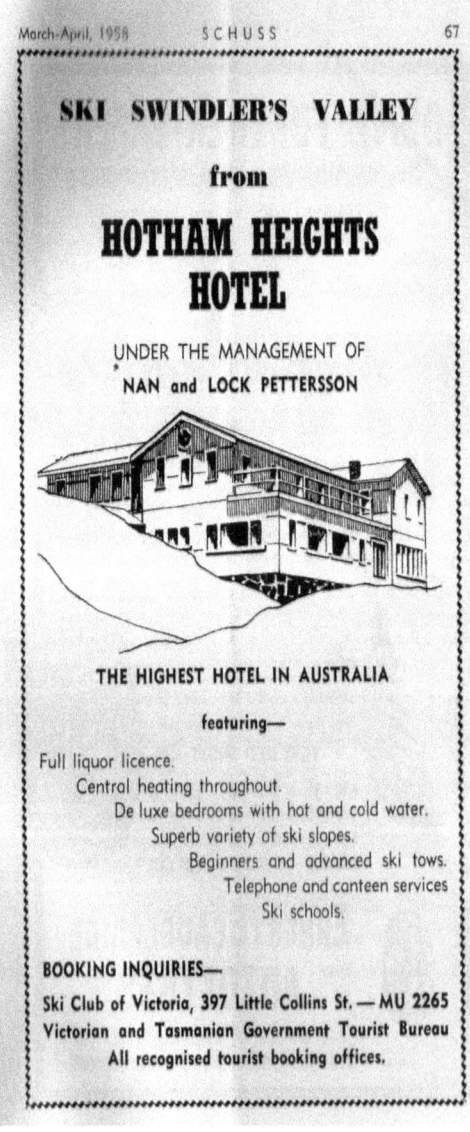

Schuss, March-April 1958

Pearl looked for the leaf-shaped scar on her arm, a legacy of the 1939 fire, while I was interviewing her, but found that it had faded away and was no longer visible.

I was in communication with Peter at around the time of the interviews, but lost touch shortly after. Efforts to reestablish contact with Peter or his descendants in recent times have proved unsuccessful.

Pearl Isabel Bradshaw died in 2001, at the age of 91. She was buried beside her husband, James Noble Bradshaw, in the Fawkner Cemetery.

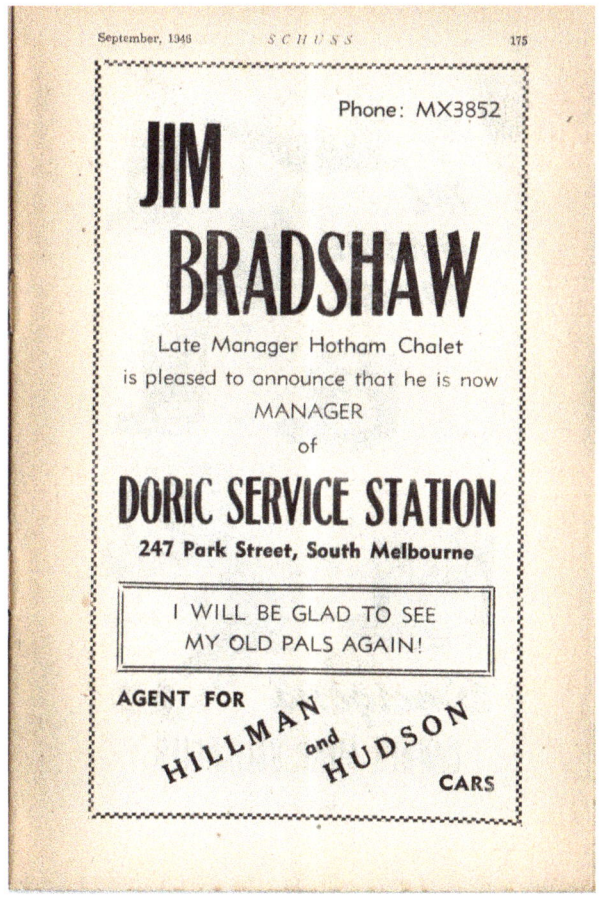

Schuss, December 1946

The People

Vic Wraith

Vic (Francis Victor) Wraith was one of two sons born to Frank and Annie (nee Gow) Wraith. (The other son was Carl.) The Wraiths were a household name in Harrietville. Frank ran the general store for many years. He was also a Justice of the Peace. Frank was one of eleven children born to Henry and Marian (nee Barber) Wraith, who emigrated from England independently, and met in Beechworth. Henry worked as a gold miner in Beechworth and Ballarat, then Beechworth again, before the couple moved to Harrietville.

The Bradshaws were not the first people to be rescued by Vic Wraith. The Argus reported in 1935 that in August of that year Vic had arranged for packhorses to meet a group that were carrying out on a stretcher, through deep snow, Mr Frank Janesse, who had injured his ankle while skiing at Mt St Bernard. No doubt there were many others.

'Ding' Dyason

Diana Joan 'Ding' Dyason (1919-1989) was born to a wealthy family in Sandringham, Melbourne. She studied science at Melbourne University, majoring in physiology and bacteriology. She then embarked on a career as an academic, performing roles as both a researcher and a teacher.

As a researcher she performed important work furthering our understanding of malaria, of key importance in the wake of World War 2. Under the headline, 'MALARIA RESEARCH NEEDS WORMS', the (Melbourne) Sun News-Pictorial of Monday, 12th August 1946, carried the following small article:

Returned servicemen suffering from malaria will benefit if a large supply of "meal" worms reaches Miss Diana Dyason at the University immediately. She is conducting experiments on about 60 bats, which live on meal worms, moths or any large juicy insect. The ordinary earth-worms are useless. The meal worm, found in quantity under old sacks or in rotting vegetation, is shiny yellow-brown or black, and has a hard skin with six legs in front, and none at the back.

Dyason worked closely with Professor Roy Douglas ('Pansy') Wright, professor of physiology at the University of Melbourne. (It was Wright who sounded the alarm on the hazards of alcohol in the snow, following the tragic deaths of three people on the Staircase Spur, Mt Bogong, in 1943.)

However, it was as a teacher that Dyason really shone. She developed an interest in the history of science. One of her courses, 'Glorious Smelbourne', was conducted in collaboration with the folk singer Danny Spooner. In the early 1950s, she had an extended period of leave due to a skiing injury. In 1967 she was appointed foundation president of the Australasian Association for the History and Philosophy of Science. Her entry in the Australian Dictionary of Biography states that

her lack of respect for authority was regularly reported, and was a characteristic she never entirely lost.

Is that why she was always late for breakfast at Hotham? It also says:

Although she often seemed to be acting amid barely controlled chaos, students appreciated Dyason's dedication and generosity... Outside the university, she wrote poetry, painted in watercolours, and enjoyed bush-walking.

Writing in 'The Half-Open Door - Sixteen modern Australian women look at professional life and achievement', she said:

The winter views from Mt Buller were wonderful, but the snow-covered ranges as seen from Mt Hotham had a spaciousness and magic all their own.

Kath Magill

Kath Magill (1903-1986) was a pioneering skier, and prominent racer. She was a member of the Ski Club of Victoria, and a founding member and secretary of the Australian Women's Ski Club. She was also an excellent photographer, and presented her photographs beautifully in albums that are now held by the State Library of Victoria. They provide an invaluable record of the early days of the Victorian skiing industry.

GAY FIGURE IN THE SNOW

WEARING a gay Tyrolean hat covered with ski club badges, Kath Magill, of the Victorian Ski Club, lights a cigarette after a run at Mt. Buller, where the ski-ing season opened during the weekend.

Bill Spargo

Bill Spargo

William Benjamin ('Bill') Spargo (1888-1959) - always addressed by Pearl as 'Mr Spargo' - was born in Bairnsdale. In 1921, he was appointed head of the road gang charged with the task of resurrecting the rundown Alpine Road that ran over Mt Hotham from Omeo to Harrietville. In 1925, the Country Roads Board (CRB) built a stone cottage on the saddle between Mts Hotham and Higginbotham to house Bill and his co-workers. Bill persuaded the CRB to allow him to take in paying guests during the winter months. Thus was born the Hotham ski resort.

However, in 1933 the Victorian Railways took over the management of the cottage (now known as the 'Hotham Heights Chalet'), and Bill's lease was terminated. His real passion was gold prospecting, and he built a one room hut at the end of Golden Point, on the opposite side of Swindlers Valley, where he lived for many years. He survived the 1939 fire in this hut.

In 1940, he discovered a rich gold reef, 'The Red Robin.' (Prior to this he had worked as a 'useful' for the Bradshaws at the Chalet.) In 1941, the Red Robin yielded 137 ounces of gold from two tons of hand-picked ore. He was offered £60,000 by BHP, but refused to sell.

Bill's long-term partner, the English-born Evelyn Piper, had returned to England in 1938. She came back to Australia in 1946 to marry Bill. Pearl had no clear memory of Evelyn. She thought she might have met her once or twice.

In 1952, Bill and Evelyn separated. They sold the Red Robin Mine. Evelyn returned to England. Bill retired to Point Lookout on North Stradbroke Island in Queensland, where he lived in a style very similar to what he had lived in Victoria.

On one occasion before making the final move, Bill was forced to travel to Queensland quickly. There was no option but to fly. He spent the night with the Bradshaws at their house in South Melbourne. According to Pearl, Bill had always been terrified of aeroplanes, and had gone out of his way to avoid them. He said to her:

"Mrs Bradshaw, if anything should happen you would be a witness, wouldn't you, that I was on that plane."

Pearl was amazed that his fear was so deep. She was equally amazed at his change of heart following his return, when he commented on his experience of flying in the following way:

"It's something everybody should do before they die, if they have to save all their lives for it."

Spargo's Hut at Golden Point is located within the Hotham resort boundary. I successfully nominated Spargo's Hut for registration with the Historic Buildings Council - now Heritage Victoria - in 1988.

Spargo's Hut with the fog coming in

Joyce Brockhoff

Joyce Brockhoff was another early skiing pioneer. She first represented Victoria in interstate skiing in 1933, and was captain of the Victorian team in 1939.

Born Joyce Johnson, she married Alan Brockhoff (of the famous biscuit-making family), the middle son of Frederick and Lola Brockhoff, at St John's Church, Toorak, in 1932. She was a Vice-President of the Australian Women's Ski Club, and an active participant in the club's programme to stock and maintain the libraries on Australian hospital ships during World War 2. She was also a Red Cross transport driver.

Joyce Brockhoff died in 1947. The Joyce Brockhoff Memorial Cabin was erected by the Australian Women's Ski Club in 1949. It is situated on one of her favourite ski runs. Writing in the Australian Ski Year Book of 1950, Mrs Dorothy Broatch (better known as 'Dot' Tickle) stated that Joyce Brockhoff was "beloved by all for her personal charm and great sportsmanship."

The Joyce Brockhoff Memorial Hut, as it was in 2016
It now operates as a cafe, "Hoff Hut", during the snow season.

'Mr Whatmore'

Mr W Whatmore was the CRB patrolman for the Alpine Road during the time the Bradshaws managed the Chalet. He was based at Cobungra (between Mt Hotham and Omeo). I don't know his first name.

The view from the Joyce Brockhoff Memorial Hut

Harold Brockhoff

Harold Brockhoff was another early skiing pioneer, and member of the Ski Club of Victoria. Born in 1902, he was the oldest of the three sons of Frederick and Lola Brockhoff. Like his brother, Alan (who was in charge of manufacturing), he worked for Brockhoff Biscuits. The relaxed, extraverted Harold oversaw marketing. Brockhoff Biscuits advertised extensively in Schuss and the Australia and New Zealand Ski Year Books.

"A Sunbath at Mt. Hotham."

Bruce Wenzel

Bruce Wenzel was another early skier. In later years, he became the Foundation President of the Koomerang (Scotch College) Ski Club. He served as President from 1957 - 62. Scotch College and Melbourne Grammar competed against each other in snow skiing in 1957. This was the first competition between two schools.

The Bruce Wenzel Interschools Trophy, awarded to the winning boys' team from 1958 - 2006
Photographer: Mark Ashkanasy; Source: National Alpine Museum Australia Collection

Lindsay Salmon

Lindsay Salmon (1914-1973) was another pioneering skier. He was a foundation member of the Albury Ski Club. According to his daughter, Gillian, writing in her book 'The King of Hotham *My Father*', Salmon joined the Australian Armed Forces on 5th November 1939. He spent a gruelling time fighting in the Middle East before joining the 1st Australian Corps Ski School in 1941, helping to train soldiers to ski in the mountains of Lebanon. Although, as it turned out, skiing soldiers were never used in combat in World War 2, the experience was once again extremely taxing, with the heaviest falls of snow seen in the area for thirty years. The hotel the troops were staying in was snowed in. The telephone line went down. The electricity failed, causing a loss of lighting and heating. The water pipes froze, and food ran very short. It was during this time, Gillian tells us that, in spite of these great difficulties (or perhaps because of them, and the satisfaction that came from meeting them), Salmon first began to dream of building his own chalet. He returned to Australia early in 1943, and spent the winter of that year convalescing at the Hotham Heights Chalet.

Salmon began advertising his services as a skiing instructor in Schuss in February 1947. His chalet, 'The Drift', opened for business at Hotham in 1951, only the second site of commercial accommodation on the mountain. Lindsay Salmon, skiing instructor and guest house operator, was a powerful presence for many years at Mt Hotham. He died following a car accident in Porepunkah at the age of 58.

Memorial to Lindsay Salmon near the summit of Mt Higginbotham (this page and the following page)

Lindsay Salmon's 'Drift' Chalet, as it is in 2025
It is now owned by CSIR Ski Club.

Noel and Joan Dickson

Noel (1907-1984) and Joan (nee Purnell) Dickson were both also very early skiers. They were married in 1940. Beyond this, I have not been able to find out much about them. I do know that the Wendix ski run at Hotham was named after Bruce Wenzel and Noel Dickson. As I mentioned in the Introduction, I spoke to Joan briefly on the phone in 1987. She was an important link in the chain of communications that led me to Pearl.

This memorial to Eric Johnson stands beside the Alpine Road near Diamantina Hut.

Eric Johnson

Eric Gravbot Johnson was born in Norway. He emigrated to Australia as a young man after a falling-out with his father. He never returned. Johnson was an expert skier, but very rough and ready. His skis appeared to be home-made, and barely even turned up at the front. When he landed after a jump (he was an excellent jumper), they threw up great spumes of snow. He suffered from severe eczema on his hands, which created deep cracks upon his palms. Rather than wearing gloves or mittens, however, he wore socks full of holes on his hands.

Johnson worked for Bill Spargo at the Red Robin Mine, but the two men did not really get on very well. He also worked for Martin Romuld on the preparatory stages of the Kiewa hydroelectric scheme. He had a team of horses and, following an idea developed in Norway, he fashioned snowshoes for them. In 1943 he employed these with great success to sledge in the meat supply for the Hotham Heights Chalet. Encouraged by this, the following year he brought in the luggage of the skiers over the snow. The skiers loved his service, but he drove his horses very hard. Many found it distressing to watch them floundering in the deep snow, and there was much debate as to whether his treatment of his horses was reasonable or not. Pearl and Jim felt he crossed the line.

The plaque reads in part:
COURAGEOUS FRIEND OF STRUGGLERS IN THESE MOUNTAINS WHEN TRAVEL WAS ON FOOT AND HORSE OFTEN IN FOG AND BLIZZARD SEARCHER AND HELPER FOR ANY IN DISTRESS REGARDLESS OF HIS OWN PERSONAL SACRIFICE

Vic Lawler

Vic Lawler (1895-1962) was the sixth of seven sons of John and Ellen (nee O'Rourke) Lawler. There were also four daughters. The Lawlers held cattle leases in the Victorian high country for many years. Vic was particularly known for also being a very proficient axeman and timber cutter. Like most of the cattle families, the Lawlers built a rough hut to serve as a base during the summer, when their cattle were grazing in the mountains.

There were actually three Lawlers Huts. The highest of these was on the saddle between Mts Hotham and Higginbotham, just behind the original Hotham Heights Chalet. This hut, and Maddisons Hut at Mt Bogong, were the two highest cattlemen's huts in Victoria.

In the early days of Victorian skiing, Lawlers Hut at Hotham often held overflow from the Chalet. Bill Spargo lived there during the winter of 1933. This hut was burnt down in the bushfire of 1939. When the Victorian Railways rebuilt the Chalet, they erected three simple huts nearby to house the construction workers. When the workers left, one of these huts was left standing to serve as a new hut for the Lawlers. They paid £5 for it. Eventually it became very rundown, and was demolished in the 1960s.

The Places

This sculpture in memory of Bill Spargo's Red Robin Mine (this page and the following page) was created by mining heritage expert and artist Andrew Swift, and once stood at the Mt Loch car park. It is no longer there.

The Red Robin Mine

Bill Spargo discovered the rich Red Robin gold reef on Machinery Spur near Mt Loch in 1940. The find triggered Victoria's last significant gold rush. Bill and Evelyn sold the Red Robin Mine to Norm and Lilian Staff of Harrietville in 1952. It passed through a series of owners before eventually being closed under government direction in 2014. It is situated within the Alpine National Park, and is now registered with Heritage Victoria. It is the only intact alpine gold mine in Australia.

The Bogong High Plains

The Bogong High Plains lie in northeast Victoria, in the heart of the Victorian Alps. Mt Bogong, Victoria's highest mountain, lies to their north, Mts Hotham and Loch lie to their south, and Mts Feathertop and Fainter to their west. The High Plains contain two man-made lakes, constructed for the Kiewa Hydroelectric scheme. The Pretty Valley Pondage was created in the 1940s, and the much larger Rocky Valley Dam was completed in 1959. Falls Creek ski resort lies within the Bogong High Plains.

For many years, cattlemen used to bring their cattle up to Victoria's high country in the spring to graze on the lush pastures during the summer months. They would return in autumn to muster the cattle, and take them back to the valleys before the arrival of the winter snows. Often cattle belonging to different families would become mixed, and need to be separated. Harry Stephenson, who has written extensively on the subject, says that the Bogong High Plains cattle muster was Victoria's most complex, involving cattle from fourteen different leaseholders. Cattle grazing was banned on the Bogong High Plains in 2015, for environmental reasons.

Wallaces Hut

Wallaces Hut was built out of local timber over six weeks in 1889 by three brothers, Arthur, William and Stewart Wallace, who had emigrated from Ireland. They held leases for grazing cattle on the Bogong High Plains. The hut was built to provide shelter for them, and has also provided shelter for many others over the intervening years. Wallaces Hut was also used by the State Electricity Commission in the first half of the last century to gain precipitation data for future potential hydroelectric projects. It is generally regarded as the oldest surviving hut on the High Plains, and is probably the only one from the 19th century. Wallaces Hut is registered with Heritage Victoria.

Wallaces Hut, as it was in 2014

Cope Hut

Cope Hut was built at Middle Creek near Mt Cope, on the Bogong High Plains, in 1929. It was proposed by R W Wilkinson on behalf of the Ski Club of Victoria as a refuge for skiers, as the cattlemen's huts were thought to be too rundown to serve as proper winter refuge, and funded by the State Tourist Committee.

Bill Spargo chose the site for the hut, but was criticised for choosing a position with little available wood. There were other problems, too. The water supply proved troublesome, and snow banked up heavily against the front door. In spite of these difficulties, however, it became very popular. Martin Lawler built the hut, assisted by his son, Jack, and his cousin, Bill Farrington. It was described as follows in the Ski Club of Victoria Year Book of 1930:

The Cope Hut...is, without a doubt, the most comfortable hut yet erected for the convenience of ski-runners.

Cope Hut was known as 'The Menzies of the Plains' after the Hotel Menzies, Melbourne's most luxurious hotel at the time.

Cope Hut, as it was in 2014

The 1939 Bushfires

The bushfires that took place in Victoria over the summer of 1938/39 burnt out almost two million hectares of land. Seventy-one lives were lost. A Royal Commission was subsequently held into the fires. It reads in part:

...the numerous fires...reached the climax of their intensity and joined forces in a devastating confluence of flame on Friday, the 13th January.

On that day it appeared that the whole State was alight. At midday, in many places, it was as dark as night. Men carrying hurricane lamps, worked to make safe their families and belongings. Travellers on the highways were trapped by fires or blazing fallen trees, and perished. Throughout the land there was daytime darkness.

September, 1945   *SCHUSS*   197

Members of S.C.V. on Active Service

Aird, Sgt. A. J.
Allen F.O. A. E., R.A.A.F.
Asifkanasy, Major M., A.I.F.§
Austin, Sgt. T. E., A.I.F.§
Austin, G., R.A.A.F.
Bainbridge, W. R., A.I.F.
Bailey, Nurse Betty, A.G.H.
Ballingall, Pte. R. T., Field Amb., A.I.F.
Balstrup, A.C.W. L, W.A.A.A.F.
Barr, Sister M., W.R.A.N.N.S.
Bathurst, A. C., E.A., R.A.A.F.
Beauchamp, F.O. T., R.A.A.F.*
Bell, L.-Corpl. R. C., R.A.E.
Bell, Pte. R. J., A.I.F.
Bennett, Sgt. D. S.
Bickers, L.-Corpl. D. A.
Bignell, Surg.-Lt. J. L., R.A.N.R.
Blamey, General Sir Thomas.
Blamey, T., M.B.E., Lieut.-Col.
Blazeley, Capt. P. L., A.I.F.
Bowman, Lt. T. J., A.I.F.
Bradford, S.O. L. M., W.R.A.N.S.
Bradford, L.A.C. C. M., R.A.A.F.
Bretherton, F.Lt., B., D.F.C., R.A.A.F.§
Bromby, P.O. W. N., R.A.A.F.
Brown, Sgt.-Pt. D. S., R.A.A.F.‡
Buckland, A.C.1, R. V., R.A.A.F.
Buddle, T., R.A.A.F.
Burns, Cpl. R. C.*
Burroughs, Gnr. W., R.A.A.
Byam-Wright, F.O. E., R.A.A.F.
Caine, A.C.2 W., R.A.A.F.
Canterford, Sgt. E., A.A.M.C.
Carlson, W., R.A.A.F.
Cartwright, Pte. L., A.I.F.
Cato, Sqdn.-Ldr. Dr. E., R.A.F.
Chenhall, Cpl. J. K., A.I.F.
Church, A.S.O. S., W.A.A.A.F.§
Clugston, F.-Lt. A., R.A.A.F.
Clymer, W., A.I.F.
Cobb, J., R.A.A.F.
Colebatch, Capt. J., A.G.H.
Cohen, Gp.-Capt. J., D.F.C., R.A.A.F.
Colquhoun, Lt.-Col. J. B., A.G.H.
Connor, Sgt. A., D.F.M., R.A.A.F.
Corr, Cpt. V. M.
Crawcour, Major S., A.G.H.§
Crawford, Maj. J., A.I.F.
Croft, F.Sgt. V., R.A.A.F.
Crowle, Capt. G. M., A.I.F.
Cullen, M., Field Ambulance.
Cuzens, Sgt.-Pt. G. G., R.A.A.F.
Davis, Lieut. L. J., A.A.
Dawson, Sgt. R. S., A.M.F.
Denham, F.O. J. N., R.A.A.F.
Dewez, Flt.-Sgt. A., R.A.A.F.
Dixon, F.O. H., R.A.A.F.
Doggett, P.O. A. C., R.A.A.F.§
Donaldson, Lieut. J. L., A.I.F.*
Doube, A.C.2 G. J., R.A.A.F.§
Douglas, Ft-Sgt. G., R.A.A.F.
Dowdle, Pte. A. J., A.M.F.
Dreverman, Cpl. W. B., R.A.A.F.
Duigan, Lieut Cynthia, A.G.H.
Dunscombe, E. W., R.A.A.F.
Ead, Pte. H. J. A.I.F.†
Eggleston, F.O. F., R.A.A.F.
Favaloro, S.-Ldr. F. G., R.A.A.F.

Fennessy, Sgt. J., A.I.F.
Fidler, Gnr. F. E., R.A.A.
Finlason, F.O. W. D., R.A.A.F.†
Finlayson, Sgt-Plt. F., R.A.A.F.
Fisher, Cpl. T. D.
Folk, J. W., R.A.N.
Gadsden, P.O. J. G., R.A.A.F.‡
Gale, L.A.C. A. D., R.A.A.F.
Garing, Gp.-Cpt. W., D.F.C., R.A.A.F.
Gerkens, Lt. (S.) P. R. d'Arnaud, R.N.N.
Gibson, Cpl. J.
Greaves, A.C.2 C., R.A.A.F.
Griffiths, F.-Lt. J. C., R.A.A.F.‡
Habersberger, F.O. M., R.A.A.F.
Halls, Driver E. G.
Harbison, L., W.R.A.N.S.
Harker, Lieut. G., Sigs. A.I.F.
Harkins, Capt. M. J., A.I.F.
Hartley, Sergt. A. E.
Haughton, Capt. N., A.I.F.
Head, Capt. E. C., A.I.F.§
Heffernan, Cpl. M., W.A.A.A.F.
Hehir, Capt. J. L., A.I.F.
Heywood, Capt. L. A.
Higgins, Lt. D., A.W.A.S.
Higgs, B., R.A.A.F.
Hindle, Major G.
Holmes, Lieut. B. M., R.A.N.
Hopkins, J.
Hoskins, Lt. K. C., A.I.F.
Howe, W.O. L. F.
Hull, P.O. C. D., R.A.A.F.§
Hull, S.Ldr. P. E., R.A.A.F.
Hulme, G., R.A.A.F.
Hunter, K., Armoured Division.
Hunter, Sgt. R. C., A.T. Regt.
Hyland, Capt. C. K., A.I.F.
Ingoldby, P.O., R.A.A.F.‡
Irvine, Sergt. F. J., R.A.A.F.*
James, Sgt. H. B., A.I.F.
Jardine, L., A.I.F.
Johnstone, A.C.1 D., R.A.A.F.§
Joshua, Major G. M., A.I.F.
Joshua, A.S.O. C., W.A.A.A.F.
Kaaten, F.Lt. S., R.A.A.F.
Kay, Sgt. J., W.A.A.A.F.
Kemp, S.Ldr. G. E., R.A.A.F.
Kent-Hughes, Maj. M. O., A.G.H.
Kershaw, Sub.-Lieut. J. W., R.A.N.V.R.
Kiely, A.C.1 J. W., R.A.A.F.
Kinsman, W. R., R.A.A.F.
Kitchen, S.Pt., D. G., R.A.A.F.‡
Kitchen, A.C.1 S. A., R.A.A.F.
Knox, Sgt. K. W., A.I.F.
Kohn, Sgt. C., R.A.A.F.
Lang, Capt. P. S., Anti-Tank Co.
Langsford, L.A.C. F. A., R.A.A.F.
Larkins, Lt. F., A.I.F.
Laycock, Capt. B. A., A.I.F.
Leask, Lieut. J. C.
Lerew, W.Cr., J., D.F.C., R.A.A.F.
Lewis, Nurse Margaret, A.G.H.
Lillistone, Pte V. R., A.I.F.
Loughhead, Cpl. F., A.I.F.
Lyall, W.O. R., R.A.A.F.
Mackay, Major A. J. G., A.G.H.
Marshall, Sergt. I. D., A.I.F.
Martin, Pte. W. A., A.I.F.

§ Discharged.   †Prisoner of War.   ‡ Killed in Action.   *Missing.

Matheson, Lt. J. A., R.A.E.
Masters, L.A.C. W., R.A.A.F.
McCaw, Capt. T., R.A.A.
McColl, F.-Lt. M. M., R.A.A.F.
McCreath, A.C.2 C. A., R.A.A.F.
McCutcheon, S.-Ldr. O., R.A.A.F.
McGough, W.O. F., A.I.F.
McLean, Capt. A. T.
Mellor, A.C.2 N., R.A.A.F.
Mellor, Pte. R. N., A.A.S.C.‡
Meredith, Lt. R. J., A.I.F.
Meyers, K.
Michielsen, Lt. K. G. P., R.N.N.
Milner, A.C.1 M. J., R.A.A.F.
Mitchell, Capt. T. W., A.I.F.†
Munro, Dvr., A. R., A.W.A.S.
Myers, A.C.1 R.A.A.F.
Napthine, F.-Lt. M., R.A.A.F.
Neil, Capt. A. C., A.I.F.‡
Neiman, Sgt. F. R., A.I.F.
Neuendorf, Capt. K.‡
Nicholson, Capt H. G., A.I.F.
Nodrum, Sergt. E. C., R.A.A.F.*
Orr, Major R. G., A.G.H.†
Parkin, Sub-Lt. G. C., R.A.N.‡
Parkin, L.A.C. K., R.A.A.F.
Pausey, F.-Lt. R., R.A.A.F.
Pearson, J., R.A.A.F.
Pern, Major G., A.A.M.C.
Petersen, J. C., R.A.A.F.
Picot, Sgt. D. A., R.A.A.F.
Pither, Ft.-Lt. R.A.A.F.
Pitt, Sgr. H. W., A.I.F.
Pizzey, F.O. J. M., R.A.A.F.‡
Plunkett, Corpl. N.
Pollock, P., R.A.A.F.
Porter, Corp. M. B.
Posner, Pte. L. D., A.M.F
Pullar, Pte. M. J., A.I.F.†
Purcell, F.O. R., R.A.A.F.
Putt, Pte. K.
Pyne, F.O. F. J., R.A.A.F.
Randall. Cpl. E., A.A.M.W.S.
Robertson, S.Ldr. K., A.F.C., R.A.A.F.
Robertson, R. W., A.I.F.
Robins, Cpl. A. H., A.I.F.§
Roe, F.-Lt. R. H., D.F.C., R.A.A.F.‡
Rogerson, Sgt. J. H., R.A.A.F.‡
Rolling, Cpl L. F., A.I.F.
Ross, Lt. J. F., A.I.F.†
Ross, F.O. W. G., D.F.M., R.A.A.F.
Rudd, Sapper W. A., R.A.E.
Sadler, Sgt. F., R.A.A.F.
Salmon, Gnr. L., A.I.F.§
Sandford, Ft.-Lt. J. D.F.C., R.A.A.F.
Sawyer, Pte. J., A.W.A.S.
Schilling, F.O. R., R.A.A.F.§

Scott, M., R.A.A.F.
Scrivenor, O.S. H. H., R.A.N.
Sealy, Major H. V., Indian Army.
Selkirk, A.C.1 W. J., R.A.A.F.
Sellers, P.O. E. C. R.A.A.F.‡
Semmens, Sgt. A. E.
Shands, Gnr. R. D., R.A.A.†
Short, Lt.-Col. M. V., A.I.F.
Silberstein, Sgt. S. P., A.I.F.
Simpson, Lt. J., M.C., Br. Arm
Sloane, A.C.2 C. H., R.A.A.F.
Smith, Major I. L., A.I.F.‡
Soden, Dvr. R., A.I.F.
Sparke, Lt. L. J., A.I.F.‡
Steet, A.C.1 E., R.A.A.F.
Stooke, Gnr. T. B.
Stogdale, Sgt. D., A.I.F.
Strang, Capt. R., A.A.M.C.
Straughan, C., R.A.A.F.
Straus, Sqd.-Ldr. N., R.A.A.F.‡
Summers, F.-Sgt. R. O., R.A.A.F.
Summers, L.A.C. M., R.A.A.F.
Swain, V.A.D., E. J.
Taylor, K., A.I.F.
Thomas, G. W., Signals.
Thomas, A.C.W. J., W.A.A.A.F.
Thompson, L.A.C. L. C., R.A.A.F.
Tobias, V.A.D. P.§
Triggs, F.O. A., M.B.E., D.F.C., R.A.A.F.
Turner, Cpl. R., R.A.A.F.
Tyler, Flt.-Lt. E. E., R.A.F.
Unsworth, Capt. H. G., A.I.F.
Vaughan, F.O. A., R.A.A.F.
Vaughan, K. M.
Vanderstoel, Lt.-Com. (S.) A. T., R.A.N.V.R.
Veall, A.C.I., I., R.A.A.F.
Veitch, Lieut. G. H., A.I.F.†
Vial, P.O. L. S., R.A.A.F.
Vial, Ltd.-Col. R. R., D.S.O., A.I.F.
Vial, F.-Lt. L. G., D.S.C. R.A.A.F.‡
Walker, Cpl. D. J.‡
Wallace, Cpl. M., V.A.D.§
Walmsley, F., R.A.A.F.
Walter, Dvr. C., A.W.A.S.§
Watts, Sgt. W. S., W.A.A.F.
Wearne, Gnr. F., R.A.A.
Weston. Sapper E. R., A.I.F.§
Wettenhall. H., R.A.A.F.
White, Wg-com. E. L., R.A.A.F.
Whittaker, Major, I. K., A.I.F.*
Wilson, Major A. J. M.‡
Wilson, F.O. D., R.A.A.F.
Winter, Capt. A. L., A.A.M.C.
Wissel, Lt.-Com. F. J., R.N.N.
Wraith, C., A.I.F.
Wright, L. A., A.A.M.W.S
Wynne, F.O. W. J., R.A.A.F.

12—ARGUS, SAT, OCT 14/44

Peter Bradshaw—"Young Man of the Mountains"

Peter is just an everyday lively, freckle-faced Australian six-year-old. What makes him "different" from other youngsters of his age is that he lives in the highest permanently inhabited house in the Commonwealth —nearly 6,000 feet up in Victoria's Alps at Hotham Heights Chalet, of which his father, Mr Jim Bradshaw, is manager.

And for a good four months each year — sometimes longer — the surrounding country is snow-covered which means that Peter learned to ski soon after he was able to walk.

It was round about this time of year, when the Alps lose their winter mantle of white, that this "young man of the mountains," who was born in the city, was introduced to his present home at the age of five months in 1938. Until he was three, however, he did not weather any winters there, being taken away at the beginning of the snow season and brought back in the early spring after the thaw had set in.

His first summer was an eventful one—a summer that Victoria will long remember because of the devastating bush fires it brought. When they were at their height — on "Black Friday," January 13, 1939—Hotham Heights Chalet was destroyed, and Peter, with his parents and the chalet staff, took refuge throughout the night in a well at the rear of the old stone building until the fires swept by. From this ordeal the babe-in-arms emerged unscathed except for a few spark burns which lightly freckled his arms without causing much harm.

In October, 1939, and again in September the following year, Peter was taken up to the rebuilt Chalet at Hotham by the route the skiers follow — on horseback from Harrietville to the snow-line, from where his father skied the remainder of the journey with Peter snuggled in a rucksac on his back. But in 1941 he skied in on his own two feet and the baby pair of ski he had learned to use the previous spring. In those days he was a quaint little figure in the snow, looking like a pixie in his red zippered waterproof ski-ing suit with a hood attached. Today, however, he dresses just like his dad in navy gabardine ski pants and a navy and white sweater patterned like those worn by the Austrian ski-ing instructors, topped in bad weather by a hooded windjacket on the sleeves of which are badges of foreign ski schools, while in the house he wears short pants and usually a Tyrolean jacket. And although he has outgrown his baby ski, which are about armpit length, he still used them this winter, flipping the too-short boards around with the nonchalance of a veteran.

Peter takes his ski-ing quite seriously, and before he goes out each day can be found waxing his ski along with the "old hands." Sometimes he sets off with a group of guests from the chalet or accompanies his dad as he carries out various jobs, and often he heads for a slope near by within sight of the house with Tiger, his constant companion, trotting at his heels. Tiger, a three-year-old Kelpie, has been Peter's playmate "since he was so small he could curl up inside my dad's pocket," and is a good-natured animal who submits to all kinds of games and romps with his young master.

Life for Peter, however, is not all ski-ing. He has to have his schooling, and is being educated by correspondence. Every week day at 9.30 he settles down at his school desk and has lessons till 12.30 under supervision of his mother, who began teaching him herself in the kindergarten stage.

The Argus (Melbourne), Saturday 14th October 1944, Page 12

Peter Bradshaw - "Young Man of the Mountains"

Peter is just an everyday lively, freckle-faced Australian six-year-old. What makes him "different" from other youngsters of his age is that he lives in the highest permanently inhabited house in the Commonwealth - nearly 6,000 feet up in Victoria's Alps at Hotham Heights Chalet, of which his father, Mr Jim Bradshaw, is manager.

And for a good four months each year - sometimes longer - the surrounding country is snow-covered which means that Peter learned to ski soon after he was able to walk.

It was round about this time of year, when the Alps lose their winter mantle of white, that this "young man of the mountains," who was born in the city, was introduced to his present home at the age of five months in 1938. Until he was three, however, he did not weather any winters there, being taken away at the beginning of the snow season and brought back in the early spring after the thaw had set in.

In October, 1939, and again in September the following year, Peter was taken up to the rebuilt Chalet at Hotham by the route the skiers follow - on horseback from Harrietville to the snowline, from where his father skied the remainder of the journey with Peter snuggled in a rucksac on his back. But in 1941 he skied on his own two feet and the baby pair of ski he had learned to use the previous spring. In those days he was a quaint little figure in the snow, looking like a pixie in his red zippered waterproof ski-ing suit with a hood attached. Today, however, he dresses just like his dad in navy gabardine ski pants and a navy and white sweater patterned like those worn by the Austrian ski-ing instructors, topped in bad weather by a hooded windjacket on the sleeves of which are badges of foreign ski schools, while in the house he wears short pants and usually a Tyrolean jacket. And although he has outgrown his baby ski, which are about armpit length, he still used them this winter, flipping the too-short boards around with the nonchalance of a veteran.

Peter takes his ski-ing quite seriously, and before he goes out each day can be found waxing his ski along with the "old hands." Sometimes he sets off with a group of guests from the chalet or accompanies his dad as he carries out various jobs, and often he heads for a slope near by within sight of the house with Tiger, his constant companion, trotting at his heels. Tiger, a three-year-old kelpie, has been Peter's playmate "since he was so small he could curl up inside my dad's pocket," and is a good-natured animal who submits to all kinds of games, and romps with his young master.

Life for Peter, however, is not all about ski-ing. He has to have his schooling, and is being educated by correspondence. Every week day at 9.30 he settles down at his school desk and has lessons until 12.30 under supervision of his mother, who began teaching him herself in the kindergarten stage.

Photo Credits

Front cover photo courtesy Ian Stapleton

Victorian Railways photo of Mt Hotham and Hotham Heights Chalet/"Mt Hotham" courtesy Public Record Office Victoria, VPRS 12903/P0001, 528/04 - Page 3

Victorian Railways photo of the original Hotham Heights Chalet/"Hotham Heights" courtesy Public Record Office Victoria, VPRS 12903/P0001, 528/03 - Page 5

"Alterations and Improvements..." Leaflet inserted into Schuss, June 1937 courtesy Victorian Railways - Page 6

Mt Hotham with the original Hotham Heights Chalet in the foreground courtesy Kate Piper - Page 9

The original Chalet, with snow gum logs stacked against it courtesy Miriam Barber - Page 9

Sir Harold Clapp courtesy Wikipedia - Page 13

"EAT OR DRINK GRAPEFRUIT"

Poster No. 161 EAT OR DRINK GRAPEFRUIT (ARTIST SELLHEIM) from PROV's Victorian Railways Photographic Negatives Collections. CITATION: VPRS 12903/P1, 519/06/Gert Sellheim - Copyright Nik Sellheim (courtesy Josef Lebovic Gallery, Sydney) - Page 14

"EAT MORE FRUIT!"

Poster No. 155 EAT MORE FRUIT (ARTIST SELLHEIM) c1930s from PROV's Victorian Railways Photographic Negatives Collections. CITATION: VPRS 12903/P1, 516/10/Gert Sellheim - Copyright Nik Sellheim (courtesy Josef Lebovic Gallery, Sydney) - Page 15

Victorian Railways promotional poster courtesy Victorian Railways - Page 16

Advertisement for Bermaline Bread courtesy History World - Page 17

Hotham Heights Chalet after the 1939 fire courtesy Harrietville Historical Society - Page 26

"Hotham Chalet, 1939" courtesy the estate of Mick Hull/1940 Australian New Zealand Ski Year Book - Page 30

The rebuilt Hotham Heights - view from the north courtesy E Head/1940 Australian New Zealand Ski Year Book - Page 32

The rebuilt Hotham Heights - view from the east (front) courtesy Kate Piper - Page 33

"ON THE WAY TO MT. LOCK." courtesy O H McCutcheon/Schuss, January 1938 - Page 34

"From Horse to Ski at Bon Accord Snow Line, en route to Hotham" courtesy Australia and New Zealand Ski Year Book 1942 - Page 44

Jim Bradshaw courtesy Ian Stapleton - Page 49

Jim Bradshaw working at the weather station - Schuss, October 1945 (contents page) - Page 52

Members of the 1 Australian Corps Ski School courtesy the Australian War Memorial - Page 53

Eric Johnson with his horse-drawn sledge courtesy Ian Stapleton - Page 62

"Swindler's Creek, Hotham" courtesy J S Ryan/Australian and New Zealand Ski Year Book 1945 - Page 71

"GAY FIGURE IN THE SNOW" courtesy The Herald newspaper Monday 16th June 1947, Page 7) - Page 79

Photo of Bill Spargo courtesy Ross and Jean Goldsworthy - Page 80

"SKI-ING demands energy..." courtesy Australia and New Zealand Ski Year Book 1942 - Page 86

"A Sunbath at Mt. Hotham." courtesy F F H Eggleston/The Australian and New Zealand Ski Year Book 1938 - Page 87

The Bruce Wenzel Inter-School Ski Trophy courtesy the National Alpine Museum of Australia - Page 88

Back cover photos

Bottom left: The original Hotham Heights Chalet/"Hotham Heights" courtesy Public Record Office Victoria, VPRS 12903/P0001, 528/03

Bottom right: The rebuilt Hotham Heights Chalet courtesy Kate Piper

Author photo (top left) by Maggie Somerville

All photos/images from Schuss courtesy Ski Club of Victoria

All the colour photographs (with the exception of the Bruce Wenzel Interschools Trophy) were taken by me.

*Every effort has been made to trace the copyright holders of images included in this book. If you are the copyright holder and wish for this to be removed or attributed, please contact us.

Bibliography

Books and Magazines

Australian Ski Year Book 1950

Grimshaw, Patricia and Strahan, Lynne - 'The Half-Open Door - Sixteen modern Australian women look at professional life and achievement' (Hale & Ironmonger, 1982 - reprinted 1983)

Hull, Mick - 'Mountain Memories - Sixty Years of Skiing' (self-published 1990)

Murray, Robert - 'Biscuits & Beyond - Jack Brockhoff and His Foundation' (Haddington Press, 2006)

Salmon, Gillian - 'The King of Hotham *My Father*' (self-published 2013)

Schuss - magazine of the Ski Club of Victoria (multiple editions)

Ski Club of Victoria Year Book 1930

Stapleton, Ian - 'Hairy-Chested History - Colourful Characters of Hotham and Harrietville' (self-published 2003; reprinted 2005)

Stephenson, Harry - 'Cattlemen & Huts of the High Plains' (self-published 1980)

Websites

https://adb.anu.edu.au/biography/clapp-sir-harold-winthrop-5657

https://adb.anu.edu.au/biography/dyason-diana-joan-ding-12448

https://en.wikipedia.org/wiki/Harold_Winthrop_Clapp

https://mountainhuts.net/bogonghuts/project-one-etym8

https://nla.gov.au/nla.obj-52798639/view?partId=nla.obj-95600283

https://nla.gov.au/nla.obj-52798639/view?partId=nla.obj-95600283

https://prov.vic.gov.au/about-us/our-blog/eat-more-fruit

https://trove.nla.gov.au/newspaper/article/11365513?searchTerm=peter%20bradshaw

https://vhd.heritagecouncil.vic.gov.au/places/153

https://vhd.heritagecouncil.vic.gov.au/places/5970

https://www.womenaustralia.info/entries/australian-womens-ski-club/

Acknowledgements

Thank you to Maggie Somerville for her ongoing encouragement and support, and for editing the manuscript. My son, Thomas, and my daughter, Lenore, continue to inspire me, and share adventures in the mountains with me, for which I am very grateful. Thank you to Ian Stapleton for sending me the front cover image (and several others), for providing feedback on the manuscript, and for helping in so many other ways. Thank you to Fiona Stanley for designing the cover. Thank you to Jenny (Salmon) Christie for giving her blessing to the title. (Her sister, Gillian Salmon (now deceased), wrote "The King of Hotham, *My Father*.') Thank you to Dr Phillip Boltin for helping me to make contact with the estate of Mick Hull. Thank you to Andrew Swift, Wendy Cross, Sarah Dyer, Oliver Clayton and Dr Michelle Stevenson (Curator, National Alpine Museum Australia). Thank you to the courteous staff at Public Record Office Victoria (especially Natasha Cantwell) and State Library Victoria. Thank you once again to Les Zigomanis, Kev Howlett and all at Busybird Publishing for helping me to put the book together.

About the Author

Stephen Whiteside has been walking and skiing through the Australian mountains for most of his life. He has also been writing for many years - mostly rhyming verse, but also short stories, and articles about Australia's history and natural environment. Many of his poems have been published in magazines or anthologies, both in Australia and overseas, or won awards. In 2014, Walker Books published a collection of his poetry for children, 'The Billy that Died with its Boots On and other Australian Verse.' In 2015, the book won a Golden Gumleaf for 'Book of the Year' at the Australian Bush Laureate Awards during the Tamworth Country Music Festival. In 2016 he judged the Secondary School Section of the Dorothea Mackellar Poetry Awards. Whiteside works as a GP in Melbourne.

Previous books by Stephen Whiteside

Snow, Fire and Gold - the story of Bill Spargo and Evelyn Piper's life in the Australian mountains (self-published via Busybird Publishing, 2024)

The Billy That Died With its Boots On and Other Australian Verse (Walker Books, 2014)

The "Ant Explorer" Parodies (self-published, 2010)

"The Brigadier's Horse" and other poems from the Western Front by Arthur Dean, compiled by Stephen Whiteside (self-published 2010)

The Paterson Parodies (self-published 2009)

Poems of 2008 (self-published 2009)

Early Poems and Songs (including "Omeo") (self-published 2008)

Poems of 2007 (self-published 2008)

Stephen Whiteside knew that Spargo's Hut in the Australian mountains near Mt Hotham had been abandoned for many years. However, when he first visited it in 1982, he got a shock. It looked like it was still inhabited. Could he have been mistaken? Closer inspection revealed that it was, indeed, abandoned. However, its remoteness had allowed it to remain crammed full of all the items necessary for everyday living. There was a bed and pillow, a table and chairs, a Coolgardie safe, pots and pans, crockery and cutlery, a cheese grater, a fly spray pump, an oven mitt, a golf putter, books and magazines, and much, much more.

It looked to him as though a woman had lived there as well as a man. Who were these people who had lived in this one room hut above the snow line, and why? He resolved to find out...

'Pearl Bradshaw - Princess of Hotham' and 'Snow, Fire and Gold - the story of Bill Spargo and Evelyn Piper's life in the Australian mountains' can be purchased at **snowfireandgold.com.au**

www.ingramcontent.com/pod-product-compliance
Lightning Source LLC
Chambersburg PA
CBHW061233070526
44584CB00030B/4101